Preparing for Christian Marriage

Preparing for Christian Marriage

Joan & Richard Hunt

ABINGDON PRESS • NASHVILLE

Library of Congress Cataloging in Publication Data

Hunt, Joan, 1932–
   Preparing for Christian marriage : couple's manual.
   Bibliography: p.
   1. Marriage—United States.   2.   Christian life.
   I. Hunt, Richard A., 1931–   .   II. Title.
   HQ734.H932   306.8   81-1770   AACR2

ISBN 0-687-33919-7

The poem "Wild Geese Fly High" by Emory C. Pharr is from the book *Wild Geese Fly High* and is reprinted with permission of the author.

Scripture quotations noted RSV are from the Revised Standard Version of
the Bible, copyrighted 1946, 1952, © 1971, 1973 by the Division of Christian
Education of the National Council of the Churches of Christ in the U.S.A.

Scripture quotations noted Phillips are from The New Testament in Modern
English, copyright © J. B. Phillips, 1958, 1959, 1960, 1972.

Manufactured by the Parthenon Press at
Nashville, Tennessee, United States of America

To our families—
  who helped us to grow
  and who showed us the worldwide
  Christian family
Through which God nurtures us
  in grace and love

Contents

Preface

The church is concerned for all couples, at every stage in their lives. This guidebook is one expression of its desire to enable couples to examine their relationships and to grow as partners in marriage.

We have attempted to be realistic about the difficulties and work involved in marriage. We especially want to share our deep optimism about the possibilities for growth that marriage offers. We see these possibilities because our hope and our excitement about the marriage covenant are based upon our faith in God as revealed in Jesus Christ and in the covenant God continues with us today.

You can use this book as a couple, in a group of couples, and as a supplement to interviews with your minister or other counselor.

In most chapters there are EXPLORE exercises that will enable you and your partner to practice the concepts and skills that are presented in the text. We encourage you to try at least one of these in each chapter.

In the back, you will find some forms for your use.

Wedding Information is to be filled out in consultation with your pastor. There are also two Premarital Questionnaires—one for each of you to fill out separately. Your pastor may ask you to complete these. If not, we believe you will find it helpful to fill them out, compare your answers, and discuss them together. These forms will enable your pastor to counsel you more helpfully, both before and after your wedding. Directions for their use are found in *Preparing for Christian Marriage*, Pastor's Manual.

This guidebook and the process of exploration and growth toward which this book points have been developed from the experiences of many married couples. We appreciate the many persons who have helped us refine our drafts into this present guide, which has been much strengthened by the contributions of the couples who worked as the editorial committee and as readers.

We hope you will find this manual useful, not only in preparing for marriage, but in helping you to grow in love throughout your marriage.

Chapter 1

What's in This for Me?
...for Us?
Reaching for Our Goals

Through these pages, we invite you into a very intimate, sometimes risky personal sharing with your partner. We assume that you and your partner will use this guidebook together. Because you care for each other as special persons, don't be afraid—your open talks can help you grow as individuals and as partners.

Exploring your relationship can be fun. By sharing your dreams, your hopes, and your deepest feelings and thoughts with your partner, you can strengthen your relationship and choose the direction you want it to take. We hope you laugh together, talk a lot, and hug each other, as you adventure into the many facets of your relationship. You may cry at times or become angry, and these reactions also will express how important you are to each other.

If this process of self-discovery is new to you, you may need to go slowly and feel your way into some of these areas. You may be pleasantly surprised by how often you agree and are able to reach out and affirm each other. You also may find that you can disagree comfortably on some matters and that you can decide to leave some questions to be answered later.

Consideration of your relationship in marriage (whether pre- or postwedding) involves much more than merely reading a book. You need time to talk with each other about what you want and about what you expect in your relationship. The main purpose of this guidebook is to help you talk together about everything that is important to each of you.

To explore your relationship, we suggest that you plan at least an hour or two for each chapter. You may need more time for some topics. Together, you and your partner can read the chapter (or parts of it) and then pause to do some of the EXPLORE exercises.

Choosing Your Relationship

As partners, you make your relationship what it is. Together, you have the opportunity to shape your lives and to grow in directions that you intentionally choose. We invite you to explore your present relationship and to discover your possibilities as a couple. In this process you will find many opportunities to express your love as you deepen your understanding of yourselves and of others.

You and your partner are very important to each other, to your families and friends, to the church, to the community around you, and to God. You are unique, and your relationship is very special. In many ways, it is different from any other human relationship. Thus there is no one right way for you to create your marriage. Together, you shape your relationship in your own ways. Through this growth you can share the fruits of God's Spirit: love, joy, peace, patience, kindness, goodness, faithfulness, gentleness, and self-control (Gal. 6:22-23). Your marriage can be a means of grace and love, for yourselves and for others.

Marriage implies a community of persons who cooperate and support each other in times of joy and in times of trouble. In a community, individuals are related to one another as friends, with common concerns and values. Just as you encourage others, so others want to support you as you shape your lives. You each know some of these persons in your families, among your friends, and in your church.

There are many more persons who want the best for you. Among them are the couples who helped to develop this guide. As couples, at times we have found our marriages to be difficult or frustrating. This is to be expected in any healthy relationship. By working through these difficulties, we have grown as individuals and in our appreciation of our partners. We continue to have fun as couples. Our marriages change because we are growing as persons and as partners. Each marriage is different from the others, although we all affirm basic values and skills that we will try to describe to you in these pages.

You are not alone as a couple. Many of the insights of the church and of Christian couples are included in this guide. Examine these carefully; try to experience them and adapt them to your situation. You may reject some suggestions, and we accept your decisions as signs of your growth. You may discover additional insights from other sources, and we encourage you in exploring those insights on the basis of your commitment to God and to each other.

There are no pat answers in marriage. In this guide we raise many issues and questions for you to explore together, but we do not give all the answers. Part of your joy comes from the exciting opportunity to create your own answers and to make your relationship all that you want it to be. It does not matter what 99 percent of other couples do or do not do in their marriages. What *does* matter is that you and your partner live your lives in ways that are most satisfying to you, as you understand yourselves in relation to God and to your community.

Your Freedom and Covenant

Deep in every person is a hunger to be unique and to be accepted just as he or she is, without any strings attached. To be loved unconditionally, just as I am, frees me to drop my defenses, to grow, and to love others. The good news of the Christian faith is that God loves us just as we are. We call this unconditional love a covenant (Jer. 31:33-34; John 3:16). It is like a guarantee that God loves us all the time, even at times when we feel most alone or unlovable.

The covenant of marriage is based upon this kind of complete love from God to us. This model guides us as each partner vows to love his or her mate, regardless of what happens. Although we as humans sometimes do not give this full unconditional love to one another, it is the possibility and the power of Christian marriage, in contrast with a mere legal contract.

We want you and your partner to experience your own freedom. Be honest with yourselves. Your decisions about your relationship are yours to make and live out, not those of your relatives or friends. Your agreement to explore together the many facets of marriage may lead you to make a covenant, or to renew a covenant, in marriage. You may feel that the suggestions and exercises in this guide presume that you and your partner will marry each other. We only assume, however, that you want to explore your relationship in greater depth, so that you can grow and make your own decisions about marriage.

In your explorations you may discover insights about yourselves and your relationship that will make a decision not to marry seem best for you. Perhaps every couple has some doubts about marriage, but persistent or serious reservations are important to consider. Your decision not to marry now, although perhaps very painful, may be less hurtful than a separation or divorce later. Whether you marry or not, mutual consideration of marriage in greater depth will enable you to make better decisions about your future.

The comments and exercises in this guide are oriented primarily toward couples who are considering marriage. However, couples who are already married may benefit even more from these discussions, since freedom and covenant continue to be important. Some exercises could be repeated after several months, offering the added advantage of comparing previous outcomes with your current views and values. If you are a married couple or in a married couples' group, you can adapt the phrasing of the comments and exercises in this guide to fit your present situation.

Meeting with Your Pastor

In addition to your conversations with each other, we hope you will meet several times with your pastor. In these pages we use the term "minister," or "pastor," to refer to the professional person with whom you discuss your relationship. This may be the pastor or associate pastor of your church, a minister who specializes as a chaplain or pastoral counselor, or a marriage counselor/therapist.

Consulting with your pastor about your marriage does not imply that anything is wrong. Neither does it mean that you must have the minister's approval to marry. Meeting with your minister suggests that both partners want to benefit from the perspective that a trained consultant can provide, as you consider your future. Most churches feel so strongly about the importance of this that they require ministers to consult with a couple before the wedding.

We suggest that you consult with your pastor several months before your wedding date, or as early as possible. If you are unable to meet with the person who is to officiate at your wedding, consult with another minister or counselor. You also can discuss wedding arrangements with your minister. If you need assistance in locating a pastor, inquire at a church in your community or write to one of the resource offices listed in this book.

Here are some possible ways to structure your conversations with your pastor. Together, you and your partner can decide how to use these suggestions.

1. In an initial get-acquainted meeting, you can arrange for use of this guide, for a couple-relationship inventory, and for other supplementary materials that your minister may suggest.

2. For most couples, it is good to plan several sessions with your minister during which you can consider in-depth topics that you, your partner, and/or the minister suggest. Some of these discussions may be as a couple and others may be as individuals. During these times you can talk about some of the topics in this guide, ask questions, and examine areas that may have been difficult for you and your partner to explore alone.

3. Plan some time when you as a couple and your minister can consider the meanings of the wedding ceremony and make necessary arrangements. The wedding service (and rehearsal, if necessary) is a major public event in your relationship. We think it is important for you to blend the discussions of your marriage and your wedding ceremony in order to express, both privately and publicly, your own covenant for your marriage. Chapter 11 of this guide offers several suggestions about the wedding ceremony.

4. Some time during the first months after your wedding, plan at least one visit with a minister. If your previous minister is not available, meet with the minister in your current community. These post-wedding visits will give you an opportunity to talk about how things are going in your marriage. You might invite your minister (and spouse, if he or she is married) to your home, or you may meet at a place that is convenient for all of you.

Learning with Other Couples

You and your partner can gain many insights about marriage by talking with several happily married couples, whom you can meet through a couples' growth group, a church-sponsored couples' class, or a marriage enrichment event. By visiting

with successfully married couples, you can observe patterns you would like to have in your own marriage as well as some that you might improve in your relationship. In most churches there are couples who would enjoy having you talk with them about marriage. We encourage you and your partner to seek them out or ask your minister to introduce you.

During your first year of marriage, we urge you to participate in a marriage enrichment experience with other couples. This might take place during several evenings or it could be a weekend event sponsored by your church. It is stimulating for couples to get together to compare their progress and to join in strengthening their marriages. Your minister may have information about these opportunities, and you can consult resources that are listed in this book.

Your Growth Agreement

Take some time now as a couple to talk about the process of exploration described in this chapter. Look over the topics in each of the following chapters to get a general idea of the direction your own discussions might take. Share your thoughts about these possibilities with your partner.

1. How do you feel about looking openly at your relationship? Some couples want someone to tell them exactly what to think and do in marriage, but we believe that God invites couples to discover for themselves the many great truths that marriage offers. Sometimes open, candid exploration may be hard or uncomfortable. We think you can cope with these risky or difficult areas.

2. Which topics seem easier to discuss? Which do you want to explore first? Begin with those chapters and use them in any order. Return later to the others.

3. It may help to have a notebook in which you can write down thoughts, feelings, comments, and wishes that occur to each of you as you explore your relationship. You also might save stories, pictures, cartoons, poems, or sayings that are especially meaningful and share these with each other.

4. Music and drama often describe relationships between a woman and a man. Talk with your partner about different types of marriages that are presented on television or in movies. Share your reactions to music that expresses a marriage or family theme.

5. We hope that you and your partner will schedule enough private time together so that you can read and discuss this book. At times, read a sentence or paragraph aloud. Your greatest growth is most likely to take place during those private

occasions when you and your partner are exchanging ideas. Sharing your dreams, expectations, goals, and hopes with each other is one of the greatest intimacies that marriage offers. We hope that you reflect often on these experiences.

Conflicts also provide opportunities for growth. Even a very happy couple will have periods of difficulty, disagreement, discouragement, uncertainty, and pain. If both partners deal honestly with those differences constructively, they can grow in new or unexpected ways. If some conflicts seem too big to handle, talk with your minister about finding appropriate help.

We Believe You Can Do It!

We know that you and your partner are able to explore your relationship. We hope that right now you will agree on the way you will use this guide. Explore topics for yourselves. Learn from the insights of others. And continue to seek God's guidance in your process of growth as individuals and as a couple.

As authors of this guide, we will enjoy sharing some of our experiences with you. We continue to view our marriage as a relationship between ourselves, our partner, others, and God. The comments and suggested exercises have been helpful to us, and we hope they will be useful to you.

In the following chapters we invite you to look at your present relationship and your future together. Talk about the kind of relationship each of you wants a year from today, in five years, or in twenty-five years. Begin creating your future now. We wish you happiness and success in reaching your goals and in growing in God's ways.

Chapter 2

What Do We Bring to Our Marriage?

To understand your partner
    . . . begin by understanding yourself.

As adults, we ask, Who am I? and we then shape it into the affirmation, I am . . . a certain way—a unique person. In this chapter we invite you and your partner to look at your backgrounds, your personal characteristics, and the values and goals that you each bring to your relationship. Since there are several EXPLORE exercises, you may want to review the general suggestions in the preface.

Explore: "I am . . ."

How do you each complete the statement, "I am . . ."? Try saying this phrase aloud several times to your partner. Each time, use a different word or phrase to describe the way you see yourself. Here are some possibilities:
I am . . .   a woman or man   successful   funny   puzzled   warm and loving
After exchanging "I am" statements, share your feelings about describing yourself. For example:
When I talk about myself, I feel . . .   happy   embarrassed   uncertain   accepted by you

---

Discovering Your Backgrounds

You are what you are today because of the experiences you have had in previous years. Each past year is important, but the most important time is *now*. In a sense, your entire past has prepared you, for better or worse, for your current relationship with your partner. However, you are not trapped by those past experiences. You can choose to change yourself. You can acknowledge the good skills and experiences that others have given you. You also can resolve to improve those areas with which you are dissatisfied.

The way you remember your past is very important for you and your partner now. We often remember in the form of stories about specific events in our lives. Why not set aside a quiet evening to share some important memories in your lives? With your partner, take time to tell some stories, listen, laugh, and perhaps cry, with a deeper appreciation of the separate experiences that each of you brings to your relationship. The next EXPLORE invites you to share memories. Many couples have found this personal sharing to be thought provoking, emotionally helpful, and mutually supportive.

Explore: Personal Experiences

Allow plenty of time—at least an hour—for this exercise. Select some specific experiences from the list below. Then take turns describing an event in the category selected. Go through as many types of events as you can. Add other categories if you wish.

your favorite food: as a child, as an adolescent, and now
a movie or play that you enjoyed
a very happy occasion
a time you succeeded
your favorite Bible verses or church experiences
an age you most enjoyed
a very funny experience
a dream you have had many times
a secret wish, hope, or ambition
when you were most angry or upset
a major sadness, disappointment, or hurt
a fear you have never told anyone
the biggest surprise you ever had
a time you felt especially loved, wanted, and accepted

As you share these memories with your partner, how do you feel? What discoveries have each of you made about yourselves through this special sharing? How are these memories related to your lives now? Affectionately touch or hug your partner to express your thanks for sharing these experiences with you.

You can view your childhood and adolescence as a continuing drama, with your family members as the cast of characters. You have influenced those persons, and they have influenced you. Which of the following relatives are in your family—parents, sisters, brothers, cousins, grandparents, uncles, aunts, step-parents, guardians?

You also have some special friends who may be closer to you than relatives. In addition, church and community groups are major sources of friendships for many persons.

Your sense of worth and your self-confidence developed from experiences in which you felt accepted, forgiven, loved, and affirmed by others. By contrast, depression and despair arose out of experiences that made you feel inadequate, angry, controlled, rejected, dominated, or unable to meet someone's expectations.

In the following EXPLORE, you can talk about some of those very significant persons in your lives.

Explore: Relatives and Friends

Select several relatives who have been or are most significant in your life. You might draw your family tree, with these names connected by lines to show family relationships. For each relative you include, describe some unique or meaningful characteristics. What do you especially appreciate in this person? What bothers you about him or her? In what ways are you like that relative?

Next, name some friends who are important to you. Share some of your impressions and feelings about each one.

In which community and church groups were you active while you were growing up? What did you learn about yourself in those groups? Did they leave you with any positive and/or negative feelings about yourself?

Describe some experiences that have given you confidence in yourself as a worthwhile, valuable person. Did those involve persons who were younger, older, or the same age you were?

Describe some negative experiences you have had. Contrast those with your satisfying experiences. Who was involved? What made each experience hurtful or negative? How do you feel now about those experiences?

Talk with each other about important relatives and friends. Describe the influence of each person on your lives today.

To Tell All or Not?

As you share these topics together, there are two gifts that each of you can give to the other. One is the gift of respect for the other's privacy. This is the kindness of *not* prying out more than your partner is ready to share. The second gift is that of listening without judging. You express your love when you receive your partner's confidence as a shared gift—neither right nor wrong, but very real for both of you.

In this context, how much of your past should you tell to your partner? Is it necessary for you to "confess all"? Probably not, although this sometimes may be difficult to decide. Here are some guidelines.

If you wonder whether you should tell your partner something that is uncomfortable or embarrassing for you, consider whether the past event can in some way directly affect your partner or your relationship now. Is the event likely to become known to your partner anyway? Why do you want to share it? Is telling your partner a way of putting him or her down, or of making yourself feel less guilty? If the event is not likely to affect your current relationship, it may be best to postpone telling about it. If you continue to be worried, discuss the situation with your minister or other counselor in order to clarify what you want to tell and what you prefer to keep private.

Personal privacy is a right of each partner in marriage. As you gain confidence in each other's acceptance and love, you can comfortably share more of your past. However, part of our mystery as persons is that we never can share everything about ourselves fully with another person—even with our spouse.

Past Versus Present

We have found that our marriage is much more the result of what we are doing now than of what was done in the past. Although you may have intense feelings about past events, you cannot go back and change them. The past is history, and your future depends upon what you are doing right now. It is in the present that we live and build for the future.

Perhaps a helpful perspective might be gained if each of you were to read this statement aloud several times:

I cannot change my past, but I *can* change the way I look at and interpret my past. I *can* deal with the feelings I have about past events. I cannot change past events, but I *can* change the meanings I give to those events today.

Individuals First: Being and Becoming

Creating a successful marriage is more a matter of *being* the right partner than of finding the right partner.

You are a complex, unique individual—a special person. Your identity, or personality, is the sum total of all your behaviors, habits, attitudes, values, and goals. Personality is both who you are and how you act—the characteristics that enable you and others to identify you as you.

For you to understand yourselves better, we invite you to look at four major areas of your individualities: your values and goals, your attitudes and thought patterns, your physical appearance, and your habits and behaviors.

Values and Goals

A value is the worth and importance that you assign to a certain belief, activity, or event. A goal is an objective you set for yourself; you then choose to do the things that will enable you to achieve that goal. You each bring your personal values and goals to your relationship. You also bring some values and goals of your relatives and of the friends you admire.

When you say that you are happy or satisfied or successful, you probably mean that you are able to reach the goals you have set. Some goals may be short-range, such as the completion of one of the chapters in this guide. Others may extend much farther into the future, such as the creation of a successful marriage or the achievement of a certain type of career position.

Some of the values and goals that partners have may fit together because they are similar. In some instances partners can hold different values and achieve personal goals without infringing on each other's objectives. When your goals conflict, then you and your partner must find a mutually satisfactory compromise.

Your actions express your values and goals. For example, the way you spend your time and money indicates the things you value and the goals that are most important for you. As you think about what you want during the next few years, you can benefit from comparing your goals and values with those of your partner.

Explore: Clarify Your Values and Goals

First, answer these questions about your values and goals. So that each partner can answer independently, let the woman answer first in the left column. Then cover that column at the dotted line, so that the man can answer in the second column. Use this code to show how important each goal or value is for you:

4 = essential for me
3 = very important for me

2 = somewhat important for me
1 = not important for me

WOMAN MAN
—— : —— 1. *become more skilled in the arts (music, photography, etc.)*
—— : —— 2. *help to eliminate racial, sex, or other prejudices*
—— : —— 3. *please my parents, friends, or others*
—— : —— 4. *earn a lot of money and be well off financially*
—— : —— 5. *get more education or job-related training*
—— : —— 6. *help others who are having difficulties*
—— : —— 7. *be successful in a business of my own*
—— : —— 8. *learn another language or other communication skill*
—— : —— 9. *travel frequently to other states or nations*
—— : —— 10. *have a steady job in a good company*
—— : —— 11. *be a manager; have responsibility for the work of others*
—— : —— 12. *have children of our own, or adopt children*
—— : —— 13. *be active in community work: service clubs, volunteer work*
—— : —— 14. *participate in church activities*
—— : —— 15. *have leisure time for hobbies, sports, vacations*

After both of you have answered, uncover the first column so that you can compare your ratings. Discuss your answers. Which of these goals is most important to you? Which are least important? How similar are your values and goals to those of your partner? On which goals do you disagree? For you to have a good marriage, on which goals must you agree?

Take some time now to talk about your choices. Give some examples of what you meant in making your choices.

Attitudes and Ways of Thinking

Attitudes are your perspectives on life—the way you look at others and at the world, including what you expect from yourself and from others. Attitudes also include the way you are likely to act toward your partner and toward others, and the way you interpret events. Your attitude is the way you respond to your values and goals and to others.

When you say that a person is confident or active, you are expressing your view of that person's behaviors. You have many attitudes concerning yourself, your partner, other people, and the world about you. Since your views about others shape your feelings and actions toward them, one way to grow is to look carefully at the way you view yourself and your partner.

Explore: Personal Views

Listed below are several dimensions of attitude and personality that can be used to compare your views with your partner's views. Be honest in answering, since this openness can help you both to grow.

It is important that you each answer independently. A second copy of this inventory is in the back of this book so that one partner can use it while the other uses the one below.

Place a mark on each line to indicate the point at which you see yourself and another mark for the point at which you see your partner on each dimension. To aid your comparisons later, use this code:

F = Female's view of self

H = Female's view of man (Husband)

M = Male's view of self

W = Male's view of woman (Wife)

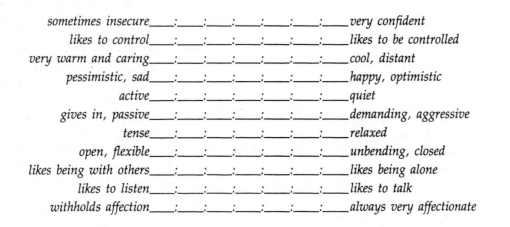

*sometimes insecure*____:____:____:____:____:____:____*very confident*

*likes to control*____:____:____:____:____:____:____*likes to be controlled*

*very warm and caring*____:____:____:____:____:____:____*cool, distant*

*pessimistic, sad*____:____:____:____:____:____:____*happy, optimistic*

*active*____:____:____:____:____:____:____*quiet*

*gives in, passive*____:____:____:____:____:____:____*demanding, aggressive*

*tense*____:____:____:____:____:____:____*relaxed*

*open, flexible*____:____:____:____:____:____:____*unbending, closed*

*likes being with others*____:____:____:____:____:____:____*likes being alone*

*likes to listen*____:____:____:____:____:____:____*likes to talk*

*withholds affection*____:____:____:____:____:____:____*always very affectionate*

Compare your answers on the two sheets, or transfer those responses to this sheet with a different color pen or pencil.

As you and your partner compare your views, try to give specific instances of the attitude or characteristic. How do you feel as you discuss these areas? If you find that you feel defensive or angry, talk about these reactions. What do you do when you feel displeased about a comment from your partner? Be open to your partner's comments and thank your partner for sharing them.

You also may talk about these attitudes and personal qualities in relation to qualities that you value, such as courage, honesty, compassion, love, and openness.

Physical Appearance

In a sense, your physical appearance is a snapshot of the visible you. Our physical characteristics enable others to identify us. Unfortunately, too often we interpret our worth or value in terms of how physically attractive *we think* we are to others. The way you dress, care for yourself, and use your body also are expressions of the way you feel about yourself.

Commercial advertising, television, beauty contests, and glamour magazines present a limited image of the qualities that constitute physical attractiveness. This image usually is presented as sexual attractiveness, with the implication that if we look like the idealized picture, we will be desired, accepted, and happy.

Your physical appearance can express your unique inner beauty, which comes from the quality of honestly being yourself. Our bodies are also God's temples (I Cor. 3:16). Through our bodies—our physical and sexual selves—we express our attitudes of love (Rom. 12; I Cor. 13). As important as physical and sexual attractiveness is, it is only one of the many rich facets of ourselves that we bring to marriage.

Explore: Appearance

Take some time to talk with your partner about physical appearance. What do you value in your own physical appearance? What do you like about your partner's appearance?

How much has (or did) attractiveness influence your meeting? How do your facial features and posture express your inner attitudes and feelings? Give some illustrations.

Look at some pictures of men and women of various ages. What do you like or dislike about each picture? In what ways are you similar to or different from them? How do you feel about these comparisons?

As you think about your face and body, what evaluations do you make of yourself? Do you like your face? Do you really enjoy your body? Do you think you are too thin, too fat, or just right? What limits does your body place on you? What would you like to change? Are you comfortable with your sexual and other pleasurable body feelings? If possible, stand before a mirror and ask yourself some of these questions as you view your body.

Personal Habits and Behaviors

Habits are your personalized way of doing things. You created your habits as you responded to previous experiences and tried to find the best ways to deal with them.

You each have routines for getting up, dressing, eating, and going about your daily activities. You have speech, clothing, and driving habits. Although you may vary some details, your habits allow you the freedom to structure your life with a minimum of attention to ordinary details. This gives you more time for planning new activities and making complex decisions. Habits are beneficial.

Personal habits are also ways to communicate with each other. Often a person is not aware of the way a specific habit affects her or his partner in marriage. Taking time to examine your habits and patterns of behavior is an important step toward greater understanding and love. This mutual acceptance of each other can form the support for changing troublesome habits. Talking about habits that you and your partner like can enhance your relationship.

Many personal habits are desirable and positive. Sometimes you may overlook giving a warm thank you for those habits and behaviors that your partner practices regularly just because she or he loves and cares for you. Telling your partner what you enjoy gives more information than complaining about what you do not like. If you know what your partner likes, then you know what you can do that will bring pleasure. By contrast, if you know only what your partner does not like, then you still must search to discover what she or he likes. Your partner needs feedback from you just as you need your partner's feedback.

Explore: Reactions to Habits

Use the checklist on page 20 to show how you feel about each other's habits. Answer separately, using the second copy of the list from the back of the book. Then compare answers and discuss details of your responses.

How I Feel About My Partner's Habits

	Very Bothered	Sometimes Bothered	Usually Neutral	Sometimes Pleased	Very Pleased
punctuality	———	———	———	———	———
appearance, dress, grooming	———	———	———	———	———
forgetfulness	———	———	———	———	———
suggestions my partner gives	———	———	———	———	———
attention my partner gives me when we are with others	———	———	———	———	———
use of tobacco	———	———	———	———	———
use of alcoholic beverages	———	———	———	———	———
use of drugs; medications	———	———	———	———	———
driving habits	———	———	———	———	———
sense of humor	———	———	———	———	———
expressions of affection	———	———	———	———	———
housekeeping, neatness	———	———	———	———	———
openness, flexibility	———	———	———	———	———
honesty, truthfulness	———	———	———	———	———
respect for others; for me	———	———	———	———	———
care of property, belongings	———	———	———	———	———
money habits	———	———	———	———	———
encouragement of me	———	———	———	———	———
cooperation, consideration	———	———	———	———	———
conversational skills	———	———	———	———	———
speech: swearing, jargon	———	———	———	———	———
sleep habits	———	———	———	———	———
daily scheduling	———	———	———	———	———
food and eating habits	———	———	———	———	———

As you compare your responses, which habits would you like to change? Most of the categories have many details. For example, sleep habits would include time to bed, time to rise, ability to go without sleep, naps, and amount of sleep required. Speech might include talking too little or too much. Eating habits could include food preferences, cooking styles, places to eat, table manners, and meal schedules.

Sometimes partners have different ways of doing things. It may be important to you that your partner accept certain habits, rather than asking you to give up what you feel is a part of your individuality. Your partner may feel the same way about some of the changes you request. One helpful approach is to clarify together in what specific way a habit or behavior causes a problem for the other partner. Then you can consider what changes you can make that will eliminate the problems and at the same time preserve your individualities.

A Role-Play Experience

The first part of a conversation between two partners is given below. Partner A believes that background (including relatives and friends) is more important than personality in influencing their marriage. Partner B thinks that personality (including habits, attitudes, and values) is more influential than background for the couple's success in marriage.

To help you explore these contrasting views, read the dialogue aloud together, with one partner reading the statements by partner A and the other person reading those by partner B. Then continue by forming your own statements to express your feelings. Try to reach a satisfying conclusion about the way your own backgrounds and personalities affect your relationship now.

A: If we can have a marriage just like my parents have, we really will be successful.

B: Their marriage is nice, but we are different from your parents and from my family. I think what we do with each other now is most important.

A: The way we treat each other now is mostly because of the way our families have treated us.

B: But my family wasn't always happy. I would hate to think that our marriage would be like that.

A: My parents have done so much for me. The way I can repay them is by being just like them. I guess I am what I have been.

B: I think my parents would want me to improve on the way they did things. My attitudes are different from theirs. I don't have to continue doing something just because I did it that way in the past.

A: Sure, but it's hard to change. When you suggest that I might change some of my habits, I think you don't understand how much my background influences me.

B: It seems that you value your family experiences and the friends you had while you were growing up. I'm glad you do. I just don't want to be stuck with the past. I have my own beliefs, and I want to do things our way, not the way someone else did.

A: Why change something, if it is good as it is? You sound as if you want to do everything differently. Do you want me to forget everything I have learned to value?

B: Of course not, but I do want us to risk change and to be aware of what we do to and for each other now. It might help if we could talk about some specifics of our pasts and our personalities and the way they affect us now.

A: That's a good idea. In that way, we could decide which things we would like to keep and which we want to create for ourselves.

Continue your discussion together concerning issues.

Each of you brings resources to your relationship that are important to understand and appreciate. Together, you have discussed some of these background and personality factors. In the next chapter we will look at some expectations about yourselves and your marriage.

Good marriages are not ready-made from heaven . . .
> A good marriage comes with some tools, but part of the instructions are missing, and you and your partner must put it together yourselves . . . and sometimes the glue doesn't stick, and parts must be changed, and new resources must be found . . . and the joy is in the search, and the creation, and the renewal. . . .

"Things will be different after the wedding." "Marriage isn't what you think it is." "I'll make my partner change after we're married." "And they lived happily ever after." How often have you heard statements like these? These types of statements express expectations.

In this chapter you and your partner can clarify your expectations about each other and about your marriage. Your expectations include the assumptions each of you makes about the things a husband and wife should do or should not do, in order to have a happy marriage. And these assumptions guide the way you treat each other.

How Couples Judge Happiness

As you have become better acquainted, you have formed many opinions about each other. You probably anticipate that you and your partner will act in certain ways. These predictions, based upon your hopes, dreams, and expectations, influence the way you view your relationship. You will compare what happens with what you expected to happen, and by this you will judge the happiness of your marriage.

Expectations have both positive and negative aspects. On the positive side, expectations provide a dependable structure for your relationship. Each of you usually knows, in general, what the other wants, likes, and will do in specific situations. This confidence gives both of you a sense of belonging and of being fully accepted in trust and love; it also can guide the way you communicate with each other.

On the negative side, when an expected response does not occur, you may feel angry, hurt, upset, confused, or afraid. You may feel trapped by inaccurate assumptions or unrealistic expectations. Unconscious expectations may limit your love and keep you from growing as individuals and as a couple.

Explore: Stereotypes

In the following excerpt, Jan and Joe reveal several stereotyped ideas as to which partner does what in their relationship. These hidden assumptions tend to shape the way they respond to each other. First, read the dialogue aloud, with each reading one part.

Jan: *As soon as I finish the dishes, let's go to a movie.*
Joe: *I would like to, but I've got to polish the car.*
Jan: *Can't that wait? We haven't been out this week.*
Joe: *What would our friends think if we drive around in a dirty car?*
Jan: *It doesn't matter that much. Don't you want to do what I enjoy?*
Joe: *Sure, but there are some things a man must do to keep this place going.*
Jan: *But I enjoy going places with you, even in a dirty car. Being with you is what matters.*
Joe: *Then how about helping me polish the car?*
Jan: *After working at my job all day and fixing dinner, I don't want to do any more work.*
Joe: *My mom never complained about helping my dad.*
Jan: *But she didn't have a full-time job, either. Besides, I do all the housework and bring in half our income.*
Joe: *Oh, all right. If the movie means that much to you, I'll forget the car.*

With your partner, identify the expectations of Jan and Joe. Here are some assumptions they may have made. Locate these in the dialogue.

Joe assumes:
A clean car is important.
Opinions of friends matter.
Jan should act like Joe's mother.
Jan usually gets her way.
Husband takes care of the car.

Jan assumes:
A clean car is not important.
If Joe loves her, he will do what she enjoys.
Jan is not like Joe's mother.
Joe will do what she wants if she keeps after him.
Wife does the housework.

How do you feel about the expectations of Joe and Jan? Talk about how you would respond to each other in a similar situation. You may write (or tape record) your own dialogue on a subject about which you have had differing expectations. Share reading the parts and then list your expectations for your own and your partner's attitudes.

Being Clear and Honest

Perhaps the key element in your relationship is that both of you continue to be clear and honest about your expectations. This will enable you to discover whether you agree on your assumptions about your marriage. As your anticipations change, you will need to have ways to talk about the changes. After comparing your views, you then can seek new understandings and agreements about your relationship. For your marriage to continue to be satisfying, it is essential that you agree on most of your expectations.

You honestly may be unaware of some of your assumptions, because they arise from experiences you have had with your parents and others in your childhood. Even if you are not conscious of these expectations, they still may influence you. This is another good reason to look at them carefully.

Dimensions of Expectations

Couples have expectations and assumptions about many dimensions of marriage. Two are especially important.

1. The Value of Specific Events. This dimension refers to the events that bring happiness, pleasure, and satisfaction. It includes affection, warmth, care, concern, love, attention, and other pleasant things.

It also includes events you would like to avoid because they are painful, disappointing, hurtful, or sad. You each decide whether a specific event is important or unimportant: whether it is pleasurable or painful; and whether you desire it or not.

A central affirmation of the wedding vows is that each spouse intends to be positively supporting to her or his partner under all circumstances and conditions. Each spouse promises to give unconditional love to the other—to care about the other, even when it is difficult to do. And each partner intends to accept the love, care, and support that his or her spouse offers. Although no couple fulfills this expectation perfectly, the covenant of mutual giving and receiving is fundamental in Christian marriage.

Explore: Affirm Each Other

Warm and sincere affirmation of each other is extremely important in your relationship. Take a few moments now to express your love to your partner. Statements such as these may help. You can complete them.
   Because I love you, I want to do what is best for you, for me, and for us.
   I know you mean well for me when you . . .
   I like the way you . . .
   When you are close to me, I feel . . .
   Because we care for each other, we can explore our expectations without fear.

A basic guide for human relationships is the great commandment to "love the Lord your God . . . and . . . love your neighbor as yourself" (Mark 12:30-31; Matt. 22:37; Luke 10:25-28; based on Deut. 6:4-5 and Lev. 19:18). This loving affirmation is both tremendously freeing and exciting, as well as perhaps overwhelming, mysterious, and difficult. Your covenant to value and love each other provides the foundation for accomplishing everything else in your relationship.

Partners as Neighbors

Your partner in marriage is also your closest neighbor and friend. Although many others have important places in each of your lives, in marriage you vow to put each other first, before all others (Gen. 2:4). You continue to care about each other in both happy and unhappy times. As you learn to care more about yourself, you are more able to love your partner. "Responsibility" means that you have the *ability to respond* to yourself, in one of these two ways:

I value and   OR   I do not
count myself.   value myself.

You also have the *ability to respond* to your partner
in a similar way:

I value and count you   OR   I do not value you
    as my spouse.   as my spouse.

These two basic intentions are continually present—reaffirmed and modified daily by what you do
and by how you treat each other. As you covenant
together in marriage, each partner can say, "I expect
to love and affirm you, and I anticipate that you will
love and affirm me."

The Basis of Your Relationship

Your continued acceptance and basic affirmation
of self and of each other underlies your view of
everything that happens in your marriage. If you feel
good about yourself, you are more likely to assume
that things will work out well for you. You also are
more likely to be independent and able to live
happily on your own. As you join together in
marriage, you can bring your strengths into a
cooperative relationship that encourages more love.

Discounting Oneself

Many serious difficulties arise when a person
discounts or devalues him- or herself. When a person
feels unloved, unwanted, rejected, or inadequate, he
or she then may set up unrealistic hopes that the
partner in marriage will provide most of what seems
to be missing in life. The discounted person then
expects the partner to give the love and meaning that
the "unloved" person feels she or he has missed.
This is a very heavy burden to place upon another
person, even if that person is one's spouse. It sets the
stage for disillusionment and disappointment, because no partner can always be giving in every
situation. It is unhealthy to expect one spouse to be
an all-loving parent, or a superservant who caters to
the other's every need and wish. Obviously, if both
partners come to marriage anticipating that the other
will "make me happy," they are certain to find
disappointment and emptiness.

You Are Loved!

But when we discount ourselves, there is always
hope. In every relationship, each partner has times
when she or he wants to be cared for—to be valued

by the other. These times need to be balanced with
times when each partner gives love, warmth, and
care. Your marriage offers you the opportunity to
grow in love. You can begin to value yourself by
accepting your partner's love for you and by
thanking your partner for that love. This points to the
second dimension of expectations.

2. The Power to Shape Events. This second
dimension refers to the amount of control that each
of you has over a possible event. Your control over
incidents in your lives depends in part upon the
resources you have and the skills for living that you
have developed. Intentional control means that you
work to achieve the goals you have chosen. You can
take charge of your lives in more ways than you may
think. You can work together to create the type of
marriage you want.

Control and Sensitivity

Control is your ability, skill, and power to cause
things to happen as you intend. But control also
includes being sensitive to the wishes and rights of
your partner and of others. When you know which
events you want—which are your goals—and if you
are able to cause those desired events to become a
reality, then you probably will feel satisfied and
happy in your marriage. You and your partner will
judge your satisfaction with your marriage by
comparing what you expect with what actually
happens.

There are also unexpected and undesired events.
When situations beyond your control occur, your
ability to see yourself as capable of overcoming
difficulties is important. When you are disappointed,
your inner spiritual resources may give you personal
strength to respond to events and to reshape your
goals and expectations. You and your partner are not
alone in those times. Your pastor, your church, and
your friends always are available to assist you in
coping with difficulties.

The ability to control your lives and your relationship can be used wisely, or it can be abused. We
believe that it is critically important for you to
discover your assumptions concerning power and
control in marriage. Since society's assumptions
about roles and power in marriage are in transition,
you and your partner need to be very deliberate and
intentional. Even the discussion of power and
control issues can generate very strong feelings.
Some skills for discussing power are presented in
chapters 4 and 5.

Expressing Power

Power is expressed in different ways. In some couples, the partner who talks more, or louder, or sulks, or says nothing, or complains tends to control the outcome of events in the marriage. With other couples, one partner may use money or sex to control certain areas. Some use subtle comments or hurtful remarks.

By contrast, power can be freeing and uplifting when partners seek a result that is enjoyable for both. Being patient and pleasant often can express a positive confidence and support of both self and partner. The old saying that "honey catches more flies than vinegar" suggests that partners can choose to use their power in constructive, beneficial ways for each other and for others. It is not a matter of whether you have or do not have power. It is a matter of using your power in constructive, rather than destructive, ways.

Sources of Power

Power comes from two sources. Some persons maintain power through their ability to hurt. Fear of the greater strength of a partner and fear of rejection by one's partner are two examples of hurtful use of power. The fear of being threatened, hurt, or rejected also may cause a person to hesitate using his or her own power. When power is based upon physical force, fear, or manipulation, the oppressed partner probably will try to escape from the unpleasant situation.

Healthy Power

A more healthful source of power is a sense of respect, love, and responsibility toward each other. As you commit yourselves to grow as individuals, your mutual sharing of concerns gives renewed power. When you really care about each other, you become free to use your power and resources in new and exciting ways that will help you to grow as persons. Accept yourself and your partner as you are *and* as you hope to be. This gives you positive power to grow.

Each of you has the power to speak for yourself. No one takes power away from you. On the contrary, you choose to give your power to your partner or to someone else. You *can* influence what happens in your life. Chapter 5 describes some ways to work out decisions about problems concerning power.

When you negotiate as to who makes which decisions in your relationship, you may agree that one partner usually will make certain types of decisions. This gives more power to that partner in those areas, but the giving of power is by mutual consent. Because of interest, time, or ability, one partner may make most of the decisions about the purchase of food, arrangement and decoration of a room, or plans for a party. When partners trust each other and share their power, the skills and interests of each can be put to maximum use in the total relationship.

Explore: Sharing Your Power

Take an hour or so to talk about the way you use your power and the way you make decisions concerning your lives. It is important that you and your partner decide openly how the skills and strengths of each of you will be used in your marriage.

First, list several areas in which you must make decisions. These may concern essentials, such as budget, money, career, having and raising children, and sexual activities. Other areas may be hobbies, vacations, and use of leisure time. Each partner may make a separate list and then the lists may be compared.

Next, talk about the assumption you each hold as to which of you makes the major decisions in those areas. To what extent does your partner control events for you, for him- or herself, and in your relationship? How much influence do other persons have over your marriage? Although others may not actually be present in your lives now, they may continue to control your relationship through your unconscious expectations that were formed while you were with them at earlier stages in your life.

In your discussions, it is essential that you seek to hear and understand each other but that you do not try to dominate or convince. You can hear the other's viewpoint without judging whether it is "right" or "wrong." Be careful not to manipulate, coerce, or force your partner, but listen carefully and try to describe to your partner what you hear him or her saying.

Some Topics for Discussion

It is important in your marriage that you each assume that you can grow, change, and shape your relationship in directions that you choose. Here are some areas to consider as you discuss your expectations and assumptions.

1. Considering your partner and yourself, how realistic are your assumptions? Is your perception of your partner's expectations accurate? To understand your partner's expectations accurately does not

imply that you always agree with them; when you express your own expectations to your partner, it does not mean that he or she must agree with all your assumptions.

2. When do you feel caught in a triangle between your partner, your parents, and yourself? Although you still appreciate your parents and other relatives, your marriage must be your primary relationship. It helps to discuss with your partner a mutual strategy to help relatives when they need you, but without allowing them to control your marriage.

3. Since expectations never are quite the same as reality, how do you feel and act when events occur differently than you had anticipated? At those times you can learn greater patience, forgiveness, and ways to compromise, without losing integrity and individuality.

4. Will marriage provide everything you always wanted, but seemed to miss? Marriage offers many possibilities, but both partners must work to achieve the *desired* possibilities.

You may enjoy considering some of your views. A few assumptions may be more threatening than others, or you may see only a part of some you hold. Keep examining your beliefs. Talk about the way you see yourselves and each other. Share your dreams about marriage. Try to pinpoint some of your specific actions that may contribute to the fulfillment of your expectations. The following inventory of behaviors may help you to study details of your relationship.

Explore: Expectations About Behaviors

The statements on the opposite page describe some behaviors that may be expected from one or both partners in a marriage. You and your partner can use this inventory to compare some of your expectations. So that you can answer independently, let the woman answer first. Then cover the page along the dotted line so the answers are out of view. The man then can answer without seeing his partner's answers.

There are several ways you can look at your answers to this inventory. First, you can compare what you each expect with what you think your partner expects. Next, you can compare "wife's answers" with "husband's answers." You also can compare your own answers with what your partner thinks you would answer. In other words, "wife's

answer" can be compared to "husband thinks wife expects." These three sets of comparisons will help you to explore similarities and differences in your expectations.

You may discuss each statement and your responses to it. At which places do you differ? How do you feel about these differences? Are there any conflicts between your four answers? How do you feel about similarities between your answers?

At which places does your partner misunderstand what you expect? Allow some time to clarify details of your assumptions. At the points where you and your partner agree, try to discover the reasons for this agreement so that you can strengthen your mutual expectations.

For each statement, indicate which partner you expect each behavior applies to. Then answer to show who you think your partner expects *each behavior applies to. Use this code to enter your answers:*

W = *usually expected of wife, although sometimes applies to husband*
H = *usually expected of husband, although sometimes applies to wife*
O = *some other arrangement, such as both partners or neither partner*
   (*After you are finished, you can describe which arrangement you had in mind.*)

Wife's Answer	Wife Thinks Husband Expects	Husband's Answer	Husband Thinks Wife Expects	
_____	_____	_____	_____	1. likes parties and visiting with friends
_____	_____	_____	_____	2. takes care of automobile(s)
_____	_____	_____	_____	3. washes dishes; cleans kitchen
_____	_____	_____	_____	4. prepares meals
_____	_____	_____	_____	5. makes bed(s)
_____	_____	_____	_____	6. suggests going to movies, eating out, etc.
_____	_____	_____	_____	7. takes care of pets
_____	_____	_____	_____	8. cleans bathroom
_____	_____	_____	_____	9. wants a night out alone sometimes
_____	_____	_____	_____	10. gives hugs and kisses often
_____	_____	_____	_____	11. likes to wake up early
_____	_____	_____	_____	12. complains about living arrangements, residence
_____	_____	_____	_____	13. starts lovemaking
_____	_____	_____	_____	14. becomes depressed, worried, or upset easily
_____	_____	_____	_____	15. fixes things around house/apartment
_____	_____	_____	_____	16. prefers to save money
_____	_____	_____	_____	17. tends to spend too much money
_____	_____	_____	_____	18. takes care of children
_____	_____	_____	_____	19. stays up late at night
_____	_____	_____	_____	20. wants more affection
_____	_____	_____	_____	21. enjoys church activities
_____	_____	_____	_____	22. compliments, encourages others
_____	_____	_____	_____	23. prefers to stay at home
_____	_____	_____	_____	24. takes out garbage
_____	_____	_____	_____	25. chooses television programs we watch

Toward Improved Understanding

In this chapter we have raised important, yet difficult issues concerning your expectations, your values, and your control of your relationship. Exploring these is risky, yet understanding each other more fully can help you to appreciate your mutual love and acceptance. Continuing to clarify your expectations takes time. Sometimes talking about your assumptions may bring surprises or even pain, but such openness gives you the opportunity to strengthen your relationship and enables you to grow in exciting ways.

I know you believe you understand
  what you think I said,
But I am not sure you realize that
  what you heard is not what I meant.

. . . Tell me you love me; it's so nice to know. . . .

Communication consists of what you say and how you say it. Both content and process are important. In communicating, being a skilled listener is just as necessary as speaking effectively. You and your partner have good communication when you achieve a common meaning, based on messages that you send and receive.

We are always communicating. There is never "no communication" between partners. When a marriage is happy and joyous, it is because the partners *are* communicating messages of acceptance, care, warmth, and concern for each other. When a relationship becomes troubled, it is sometimes because the partners *are* communicating negative messages of rejection—not because they are not communicating at all. At other times, difficulties occur because partners cannot "hear" each other because of fears and hurts from previous experiences.

You communicate by what you do, as well as by what you say. Facial expressions and body posture and position express many meanings. The tone and pitch of your voice, your silences and gestures, often speak more loudly than words, although words are very important.

Inaccurate messages or conflicting messages often occur because you are using more than one channel to send information to your partner. For example, your words may express positive affection, but the tone of your voice and facial expression may be sending negative feelings. Sometimes the same word may have different meanings for each partner at different times.

Explore: Changing the Meanings of Words

Take a few minutes with your partner and select a word or a brief phrase. Repeat this phrase to your partner several times, using various vocal emphases, voice pitches, speeds, or volumes to convey different feelings.

For example, try saying, "This is really important to me," with vocal expressions that suggest each of these meanings:

1. *You really appreciate your partner.*
2. *You actually are displeased with your partner.*
3. *You affirm your partner, whether others do or not.*
4. *You are unsure about yourself or about your partner.*
5. *You want your partner to do something for you.*

After you both have tried this exercise, talk about the changes you made in order to convey each meaning.

There are several channels through which you may communicate. Through each channel, you can express what you want, how you feel, and what you like or dislike. Sometimes a channel may express your message only partially. At other times the message may be unclear because you are not sure what you want to send. Clear messages may express affection, joy, anger, or disappointment.

Explore: Beyond Words

To examine your channels of communication further, consider each method listed below. In each category, specify a behavior and describe its meaning for you. For example, under "facial expressions," each of you may make a facial expression and then describe the meaning that you intend to convey through that expression. You also may describe expressions that do not send clear meanings to you. You may add other channels of communication to the following list:

Oral Words: *exclamations, tone of voice, volume, pet phrases, words you use often to describe many different things*

Written Words: *notes you send to each other, greeting cards, special ways of writing, symbols you use, designs*

Facial Expressions: *smiles, frowns, movement of lips or · eyebrows, angle of head or chin*

Body Positions: *posture, ways you sit or walk, position of your arms, hands, or legs*

Touches: *handclasps, backrubs, tender touches, texture of hands, hugs, other types of touches*

Space: *distance you sit or stand from each other, arrangement of furniture in your rooms*

Time: *schedules, being rushed or late for appointments, importance of time to each person*

Other Channels; *things you see, sounds, tastes, smells, ways you dress, grooming, and use of cosmetics*

Begin with the channels that are easier to explore. Continue into other channels that are more difficult or threatening. Talk together about how it feels to focus on this aspect of communication and about what you learned about each other.

Sending and Receiving Messages

It is very difficult, but *not* impossible, to change your ways of communicating. You have developed your communication patterns over many years. To change some of those habits requires time and much practice. The brief information that follows can help you examine the way you and your partner communicate now. More complete aids for improving your couple-communication skills are available. Consult with your minister about couple-communication workshops. Additional resources are suggested at the end of this book.

In communicating as a sender, your aim is to enable another person to understand your intended message. As a receiver, your aim is to understand the speaker's meaning accurately. Being attentive, open, and honest is essential in both sending and receiving. Sometimes you send messages, and at other times you listen to them. The unique advantage of a two-person unit—a couple—is that each partner can be a sender about half the time and can be a listener, receiver, and responder about half the time.

Three Steps to Understanding

Effective communication results in mutual understanding. Your communication is effective when your message is described accurately by your partner, and you both have the same understanding of its meaning. Whether your message is positive or negative, the important skill is your ability to express it so that your partner, as the listener, can understand it. Your partner then can respond by becoming the sender, while you listen. Your partner's response to your message is, itself, a new message. There are three observable steps in communicating a message:

1. The speaker sends a clear message to the listener.
2. The listener restates the sender's message by summarizing its main points. This is feedback.
3. The sender confirms that the listener's summary is accurate. If the listener's summary is incomplete, the speaker restates the message as needed, until both sender and receiver are sure they agree on the message. This is confirming the feedback.

It is the sender's responsibility to convey a clear message that is brief enough that the listener can summarize it easily. It is the listener's responsibility to attempt to summarize the sender's whole message, without adding anything to it until both sender and receiver agree on the intended meaning.

SENDER　1.— m e s s a g e　→ LISTENER
←— r e s t a t e m e n t — 2. —
3.— c o n f i r m a t i o n

These three steps result in a "shared meaning" (Miller, Nunnally, and Wackman), or mutual understanding: The sender knows that the listener has received the message accurately, and the listener knows that the sender has confirmed the accuracy of the listener's interpretation.

In most conversations these three steps are so rapid that the important feedback and confirmation steps may not be noticed. When they are missing, however, communication breaks down, or more correctly, messages are misunderstood or missed completely.

The message, feedback, and confirmation steps are especially necessary when you are sharing very personal feelings and intentions. Difficulties in communication may arise from either internal or external factors. *External* communication problems may have their source in your choice of particular words that have different meanings for your partner than they do for you. Troublesome words and phrases are like static on the telephone line while you are listening to another person. *Internal* sources of communication difficulties have more to do with your attitude toward your partner. You may assume that your partner does not value and love you; as a result, you may misinterpret some messages. At other times, you may assume that you are correct but that your partner is wrong, so you may not try to find a common meaning in the message.

Words and Meanings

Meanings are in persons, not in words. When you have thoughts, feelings, desires, and other meanings that you wish to share with your partner, they should be put into a form that your partner can understand. To do this, you package your message into words, gestures, and facial expressions, to become a message that your partner can see, hear, and touch. This is *encoding* your message. Your words and body language carry your message.

As the listener, your partner sees, hears, or feels your message and infers your thoughts, feelings, and desires. Your partner *decodes* your message to discover the meaning you want to share.

Partners misunderstand each other when they are unaware of the different interpetation given the same word or gesture by the other person. Since you each give your own special definitions to key words and gestures, these differences may lead to arguments over who is "right." Neither partner can win this type of argument. To avoid these misunderstandings, it is very important for both sender and receiver to use the same "code system." Words and other expressions that have the same interpretation for both persons aid greatly in transmitting clear messages and achieving shared meanings.

Explore: Private Meanings

With your partner, take some time to consider several "code words" that you use. Try to describe in detail what you mean when you use such words as "super," "nice," "stupid," or "ridiculous." What other words could you use in place of these, if they were not available? Talk about the way your voice and body language also can change the meanings of your common words. Give examples.

When Difficulties Occur

When you and your partner have difficulty in using the message restatement confirmation steps, it will help if you will slow your conversation and patiently state each message fully. Allow for a complete restatement (feedback) by the listener and a confirmation of the listener's summary by the sender. Usually, there is no need to be this specific and detailed. However, by going more slowly and by being sure to carry out each step, you often can locate the source of many problems that may arise in your communication process.

Practice Your Skills

At first you may feel clumsy or awkward when you explore details of your communication. This is normal, and with continuing practice you will become more comfortable with better ways to communicate with each other. Improving your skills takes a lot of effort and willingness to try.

Additional Aids

The brief suggestions in this book probably are not complete enough to enable you to make major changes in your patterns of communication. Your pastor or other counselor may have additional aids to help you practice your skills. Marriage-relationship inventories are available to assist you in looking at your personalities, expectations, and goals in several areas of your relationship. The *MIRROR: Couple Relationship Inventory* is available through your minister or counselor. Consult with your pastor about these materials and use them as a part of your communicaton-skill development.

Explore: Feedback Helps

This exercise shows the difference that feedback and confirmation can make in message communication. One partner, the sender, prepares a simple design of circles, rectangles and triangles, which can be described to the other partner, the receiver. The receiver is not to look at the drawing until after the exercise is completed. The sender then describes the design orally to the receiver, who is to reproduce the design from the sender's instructions. The receiver is not permitted to ask questions or to give any other feedback about the instructions.

When the receiver completes the design, compare it with the sender's design. Then share your feelings about not having an opportunity to ask questions or to give feedback.

Try the exercise again, reversing your roles so that the sender is now the receiver, and the receiver is the sender. Instead of drawing a design, the sender may describe an object that the receiver is asked to identify.

What are your reactions to this process? At which times did the receiver want clarification of the sender's messages? As you compare results, how do you feel? Did either person feel frustrated, misunderstood, or confused? If the designs are not identical, did either accuse the other of failure? After completing the design, do you feel more like a team? (Variations of this exercise have been developed by several counselors and educators. One early description is by Nylen, Mitchell, and Stout, Handbook of Staff Development and Human Relations Training *[Washington, D.C.: National Training Laboratories, 1967], pp. 126-31.)*

"I" and "You" Messages

"You" is a tricky pronoun. When used to identify the listener in relation to the speaker, "you" is a very helpful pronoun.

Partners sometimes misuse "you." Persons often say "you" when they really mean "I." One may say, "When you go to the store and you see the high prices, you worry about having enough money to live." The speaker here is probably referring to self, not the listener. A more accurate statement would be, "When I go to the store and I see the high prices, I worry about having enough money to live." This second statement gives a clear "I message" about the speaker's inner feelings and perceptions.

A second misuse occurs when individuals say "you" in an accusing, demanding way. Some examples: You should believe this; You're dumb; You ought to love me more; You can't be serious. These types of "you messages" imply that the speaker is demanding, dominating, or manipulating the listener in some way, and usually make the receiver feel that he or she is not valued or wanted.

Partners can replace "you messages" with non-blaming statements, such as "I wish you would believe this," or "I'm surprised." Often phrases that include "you should," "you ought," or "you must" carry underlying messages from the speaker, blaming or accusing the listener. (These concepts are based on Gordon; Miller, Nunnally, and Wackman; Narcisco and Burkett; and Pierce. For more details, consult these references in the back of the book.)

When you send a message, it contains your interpretations, feelings, desires, and plans that you are expressing to your listener. When you are the receiver of a message, you add your own reactions to the messages you hear. It helps when you use "I" to refer to your own inner self-awareness and "you" to refer to your partner's behaviors and statements. This may seem very simple—perhaps unnecessary—but using "I" and "you" in these better ways can improve your communication.

Sending More Accurate Messages

Both sender and receiver can help to make a message clear and accurate. As a sender, be sure to include these elements in your message (the exact order is not too important):

1. In specific terms, describe the situation or event to which you refer, reporting what you saw, heard, touched, smelled, or tasted.
2. Describe the interpretation (or meaning) that you give to the event.
3. Describe how you felt at the time, and how you feel now about the event. (Be alert to your hidden feelings, also.)
4. Describe what you intend or what you want to do (or not to do) as your response to the event or situation.
5. State clearly what you have decided, and the request (if any) you are making of your partner. (Don't assume that your partner knows what you want.)

Here is an example:

"When you *said* you were sorry but you *did not* reach out and hug me," (this is the specific event or message) "I *felt* confused and left out because I *thought* you did not realize how important this is for me" (these are the sender's feelings and interpretations of the event) "so I *wanted* to back off from you" (the sender's intention in response to his or her perception of the event).

Notice that "you" is used only to refer to what the other person actually *did*, not to what the other person *thought*, or *felt*, or *wanted*. The focus is on an observable event and the sender's responses to it. Of course, when the listener becomes the sender, she or he will focus on the same event and share her or his feelings, interpretations, and intentions.

Note that the better phrase is *not* "You did not realize . . . " but, "*I thought* you did not realize . . ." This shows that the speaker is reporting her or his interpretation (decoding) of the event. The speaker is not assuming anything that might be going on inside the other person, which the speaker cannot know, anyway. This statement is an example of an accurate "I message," explaining the way the speaker's interpretation of the situation was formed. It allows the listener to report his or her own views of the same event, without needing to defend against accusations from the speaker.

Listening Helps to Clarify Messages

As a receiver, you can help your partner send more accurate messages by rephrasing the words so that she or he can confirm the accuracy of your understanding. This helps the sender know that you understand how the *sender* sees the situation. As listener, you can use the same five elements mentioned before as the basis for questions to the sender, when part of the message seems to be missing. For example, you may invite your sending partner to be more clear by asking: Which events are you describing?; Did you really want that to happen?; How did you feel about what happened?

Your covenant in marriage includes mutual respect. In looking closely at a difficult situation, each of you needs the opportunity to express views openly and without criticism. If you feel mutually accepted as a team, it is easier to make the effort to achieve an accurate understanding of a situation and to gain a shared meaning.

Explore: Here and Now Feelings

Here is a way for you and your partner to clarify your feelings and your wants. You may call this your "here and now wheel." First write down two words that describe the good or pleasant feelings you have right now. Then write down two words or phrases that describe negative or unpleasant feelings you now have. These can be placed in the four parts of a wheel, like this:

Pleasant Feelings:

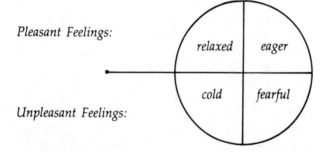

Unpleasant Feelings:

Next, write a sentence using all four feeling words, connecting them in a logical way. For example, "I am

fearful *when I am too cold, and I am* eager *to go to a place where I can feel* relaxed.*" Together you can talk about the statement you have made. Let each partner try several sets of words and phrases about feelings.*

You also may use this procedure to become aware of your values, goals, or desires. For example, enter two pleasant events and two unpleasant events that might happen, and write a sentence that includes all four. (This exercise was suggested by Gwen White, a member of the editorial committee for this book.)

Expressing Positive Feelings

Please Do That Again . . . I Like It!

The expression of positive feelings toward your partner creates warmth and a common unity that strengthens your lives together. When you share positive feelings, you not only tell your partner how you feel about her or him, but you also are saying, "I like you and what you are doing . . . please do that again." These positive feelings include love, care, concern, happiness, pleasure, joy, and acceptance.

You can express positive feelings of care and affection in many ways by smiling, touching, and talking with your partner. Being on time for appointments and planning time together show appreciation for each other. You show you care when you help your partner reach her or his goals. Sexual activities also are opportunities to share positive feelings, and humor and laughter express your joy and satisfaction.

Explore: Positive Feelings and Self-Esteem

Self-esteem is feeling good about oneself. Your sense of self-esteem (or self-worth) is closely related to the positive feelings that others express toward you. Your experiences in childhood, with friends and relatives now, and with your partner, greatly influence the way you feel about yourself and the way you express positive feelings toward others. Together, take some time to consider each of these sources.

Childhood Family: *How did family members express positive feelings toward each other? How did they react toward you? Describe some examples to your partner and compare the way each of your families communicated support, acceptance, love, and appreciation toward you.*

Friends and Relatives Now: *Name some friends and relatives who have helped you build confidence in yourself, thus improving your sense of self-worth. Talk with your partner about some specific ways each person has encouraged you. What common themes do you discover as you compare your experiences together?*

Your Partner: *Describe to your partner some things she or he does that help you to feel good about yourself. Give some words and phrases that express positive feelings you would like to share with your partner. At which times would you like your partner to express more care or support for you? As your partner asks for your affection and support, show or describe the positive feelings you have for him or her. Talk about a recent time when you and your partner laughed heartily together.*

Expressing Negative Feelings

Negative feelings refer to personal feelings that separate us from others or that reduce our sense of self-worth. Negative feelings are not "bad" in the sense that you should ignore, suppress, or cover them up. Negative feelings are your way of saying to yourself and to others, "Something is wrong. . . . I interpret an event or situation as threatening me in some way. When this happens, I feel angry, insecure, afraid, or sad." Negative feelings also can be a way to say, "I care about you, and I don't want these negative feelings to come between us."

Some of your negative feelings are temporary and will fade away as you and your partner go on to enjoy pleasant times together. You probably have other negative feelings that are more persistent. If these feelings continue in your relationship, you will need to find ways to express them and to cope constructively with their causes.

There are three basic ways to cope with persons or situations to which you attach negative feelings:

1. FLIGHT: Moving away from a threatening situation puts more distance between you. Physical distance is a protection against the threat, but sometimes emotional distance can provide a similar defense by changing your relation to the threat. Usually, fleeing from a threat restores your sense of safety by putting you farther away from the danger. However, it does not deal with the problem, because flight reduces the contact you have with the other person(s) or thing(s) involved. Some examples of flight are turning your back, walking away, pouting, emotional withdrawal, coldness, and depression.

2. FIGHT: When you fight the threat, you move against the person or situation in an attempt to

reduce its ability to hurt you. Hostile, aggressive behavior is your attempt to reduce the threatening power of the person or thing and to control it, in order to become safe and secure. You may fight physically, or verbally, or in more subtle ways. Some examples of fight are physical aggression, name-calling, noncooperation, taking revenge, shouting, swearing, destroying property, and hurting oneself.

3. REORIENTATION: Some threats, along with your fear and anger toward them, will dissolve or disappear when you look at them from a different point of view. For example, the fear that you are lost disappears when you locate familiar markers. The fear of being alone can change to joy when you realize that your partner really does care about you. Sometimes you can remove threats by changing your expectations or your goals. Usually, reorienting yourself to the situation is the most constructive way for partners to deal with negative feelings, because it enables you to continue in contact with each other and to develop the strength and skill to cope with threats to yourselves and your relationship.

Negatives About Negatives

Negative feelings with which you respond to a specific situation or person usually are called *primary* feelings. You also have emotional responses to the feelings themselves. For example, you may feel guilty about being angry, or you may feel sad about feeling alone. These *secondary* feelings then make it more difficult for you to return to the original threat or troubling situation.

In order for you to move beyond these secondary feelings, another person, such as your partner, needs to reach out to you and *accept you and your primary feelings just as you are.* This is the grace of your relationship, and it enables you to remain fully aware of the real you, without repressing or covering up parts of yourself.

Helpful Negatives

Negative feelings can be very useful because they alert you to threats and strains that need to be modified in order to preserve yourself and your relationships with others. The communication skills that you use to express positive feelings can be adapted to enable you to become aware of and to express negative feelings.

Explore: Negative Feelings

Arrange a relaxed time together to talk about the way each of you handles your negative feelings. These questions may guide you:

1. *Which are more difficult for you to express—negative feelings or positive feelings?*
2. *How often do you each use flight, fight, and reorientation to cope with threats and negative feelings? Describe a recent incident when you used one of these methods with your partner. If you could relive the situation, in what ways would you act differently?*
3. *What are some of your secondary feelings about other primary feelings? Tell your partner about a recent time when you realized that she or he really accepted you and your feelings and interpretations and allowed you to really be yourself. In what ways did this free you to better cope with your negative feelings?*
4. *Describe the way your family members express negative*

feelings. To what extent do (did) they strike things or persons, gripe, fuss, curse, nag, or complain? When were they passively aggressive by being cold, aloof, silent, or uncooperative? When do they use positive ways to cope with negative feelings, such as calmly describing a situation and their feelings about it? Which of these do you now use with your partner?

5. *With your partner, identify your negative feelings about a situation and attempt to trace them to possible underlying fears that you will be rejected, unloved, or devalued by the persons involved. Discuss together what you find.*

It is easier for some couples to be more explicit when they write their answers to these questions. If you and your partner prefer this, first write your responses independently and then find time to talk together about those statements you are comfortable in sharing with each other.

There Is More to Communicating

In this chapter we have suggested very briefly some of the important factors of good communication between you and your partner. There are many more, yet books are inadequate to assist you in changing your basic communication habits. We encourage you to participate in couple-growth opportunities that are available through churches and other community sources. Your minister or counselor can suggest couple enrichment opportunities, and you also may request information from the offices listed in the back of this book.

A Special, In-depth **Explore** Opportunity

This exercise is designed for couples who would like to examine details of the way they communicate. It will require at least an hour, an audiotape recorder, and privacy.

First, tape ten or fifteen minutes of your conversation on one or more topics of your choice. If you are not familiar with tape recording, you may need a few brief practice trials so that you can adjust the equipment and become more comfortable with the recording process.

Second, replay the tape all the way through. Notice the way you use the elements of communication when you are

the sender and when you are the listener. Listening to the whole tape can help you recover from the possible initial shock of hearing your own voices.

Third, replay the tape and use the checklist to rate yourselves in your taped conversation. A second copy of the checklist is in the back of this book so that you each can rate your tape independently. Rate yourself and your partner in the appropriate columns. The statements are phrased to apply to either partner, as sender and as receiver of messages in the taped conversation. After responding to the statements, you and your partner can compare judgments.

Use the following code:

> *1 =* not *aware of this in my taped conversation*
> *2 = aware of this but did not do it at all*
> *3 = did this some but could have done it more*
> *4 = did this well, satisfactorily*
> *5 = did this very well, as often as needed*

Rating of

WOMAN	MAN	WHEN PERSON *SENT* MESSAGES (PERSON AS SENDER)
——	——	1. *Sender was completely clear about message to be sent.*
——	——	2. *Sender checked with listener to be sure she or he was ready for message before sending it.*
——	——	3. *Sender used words that had same meaning for listener as for sender.*
——	——	4. *Sender stopped speaking occasionally to be sure listener was receiving accurate message.*
——	——	5. *Sender was open to feedback and encouraged listener to ask that message be repeated or clarified.*
——	——	6. *Sender easily distinguished between his or her message and the reactions of the listener to the message.*

WOMAN	MAN	WHEN PERSON *RECEIVED* MESSAGES (PERSON AS RECEIVER, LISTENER)
——	——	1. *Listener encouraged sender by being willing to listen.*
——	——	2. *Listener turned and faced sending partner, looked at him or her.*
——	——	3. *Listener put other thoughts aside and gave full attention to sender and message.*
——	——	4. *Listener placed own emotional reactions aside in order to become fully aware of partner's feelings and meanings.*
——	——	5. *Listener summarized message as feedback, so that sender could confirm accuracy of listener's understanding of message.*
——	——	6. *When message was unclear or came too fast, listener stopped sender and asked him or her to repeat or clarify message.*
——	——	7. *When sender paused or was unable to find "the exact word," listener waited patiently, speaking only if requested.*
——	——	8. *Listener kept sender informed of listening levels by informing sender when he or she wanted to give feedback, send a reply, or continue to receive more messages.*

When you complete the checklist, identify specific points at which you could have improved the taped conversation.

Talk about your insights and feelings during this exercise. If possible, rate and discuss another taped conversation.

Your ways of communicating express the covenant that you make as partners in marriage. Techniques are important, yet your attitudes and love for each other determine the way you will use your skills for communicating. Good communication skills are basic to your growth, and problem solving is one of the major ways in which you grow as individuals and as a couple. In the next chapter we will consider changes and your resources for shaping those changes in ways that are acceptable to both of you.

Chapter 5

All Couples Change—
And It's Tough!!

. . . Grant that I may not so much seek
  to be consoled, as to console
  to be understood, as to understand
  to be loved, as to love . . .
  Prayer of St. Francis of Assisi

It is great to be alive, and being alive means change. Change is inevitable, but growth is intentional. Old habits, like old clothes, no longer fit as they did. In your growth as partners, the resources of your church, your friends, and others can help you as you develop your lives. Because of your covenant as partners, you can look at problems and crises as challenges for growth.

In your wedding vows, you covenant to care about each other and to give and receive love and understanding. In the context of God's grace, forgiveness, and love for you, you vow to trust, forgive, and accept each other *as you are,* even when you may not feel able to do so. This means that at times you may be angry, or you may feel like running away from each other, but you will not give up. It means that instead, you will try to grow toward tenderness, understanding, and a renewal of your relationship.

This basic covenant is tremendously freeing and exciting. It is easy to follow during your happy times together. During times of difficulty and problems, however, this covenant seems overwhelming, mysterious, and perhaps impossible. There are many couples who have given up, but there also are many who have discovered much deeper levels of openness, appreciation, and mutual acceptance, as they refined their love during times of change.

Every Street Has Some Bumps

Your road to marital happiness has several bumps and a few sharp curves. Some ways may be stormy, icy, or frozen. Floods may wash out a bridge, or you may find unexpected detours that force you to change your route. As one person said, "I took my partner for better or worse, but I didn't know it could be so much worse."

If you and your partner assume that your marriage is worth your investment, then your love and understanding will give you the motivation to seek ways to resolve disagreements and difficulties. We believe that there are few problems big enough to destroy your relationship, unless in some way you *decide* to use a problem as a reason to separate.

This attitude of Christian love was expressed many times by the apostle Paul—for instance, in this statement: "Let love be genuine . . . hold fast to what is good . . . rejoice in your hope, be patient in tribulation, be constant in prayer" (Rom. 12:9-12 RSV).

You and your partner can develop this deep love as you cope with life together. At times you may need help from others. Some problems may have their roots in events that happened before you knew each other, and those problems may be severe enough to require professional help. Even a very healthy and stable person sometimes can be overwhelmed by difficulties.

There are many resources in your church and community to assist you and your partner in resolving problems and dealing with crises. The following pages suggest some basic skills for problem solving and some ways to know when you need additional help.

As you grow through a crisis, you will discover your own strengths as individuals and as a couple. This will enable you to take time to find the causes of your problem so that you can solve it more readily. The Christian approach of forgiveness and renewed relationships is a major key to problem solving. God's love works through us when we are open to each other.

Explore: Limits

These comments have invited you to consider your basic approach to each other as partners. Take time now to explore the effects that some of the following difficulties might have on your relationship. Talk with your partner about these and other issues. Share your attitudes and feelings. Keep asking yourselves, "Is there any conflict or problem that is so big, so unforgivable, so terrible, that you would leave your partner, whom you now love and enjoy?"

Here are some issues to discuss:
losing a job
spending too much money
loneliness or frustration
spending too much time with job; with others
sexual involvement with someone else
physical abuse of each other
unwillingness to talk about problems

Disagreements Reflect Intentions

Your goals and preferences will not always coincide with those of your partner. You can agree to permit differences and disagreements. Together you usually can resolve conflicts about specific issues, if you both have a basic attitude toward yourselves and toward each other that is positive, caring, affirmative, and supportive. This is not an unrealistic cover-up for those times when you honestly dislike each other and do not feel caring or positive at all.

This approach is your intent to be available to each other, to talk about differences, and not to give up.

In a conflict, partners often think that one must win and the other must lose. In most conflicts, however, it is possible for both to win. As you consider the ways you each respond to conflicts between you, you may discover some common patterns. You and your partner may assume attitudes of win-win, win-lose, or lose-lose. This EXPLORE can help you become aware of those attitudes.

Explore: Response Patterns

With your partner, consider how you each respond when you have disagreements. Listed here are twenty words and phrases that describe possible ways to respond. So that you and your partner can answer independently, a second copy of this list is provided in the back of this book.

Separately, put a check or X beside the eight words that best describe your own responses in times of disagreement between you and your partner. Answer as you see yourself.

SHE	HE	TYPE OF RESPONSE	SHE	HE	TYPE OF RESPONSE
——	——	1. withdraws	——	——	11. threatens
——	——	2. negotiates	——	——	12. pretends
——	——	3. gives in	——	——	13. looks openly at issues
——	——	4. forces own way	——	——	14. retreats, hides from issue
——	——	5. clarifies	——	——	15. begrudges, resentful
——	——	6. becomes silent	——	——	16. leaves room, vacates
——	——	7. blames someone	——	——	17. pressures, pushes
——	——	8. explains	——	——	18. surrenders
——	——	9. criticizes	——	——	19. disappears
——	——	10. evades the issue	——	——	20. compromises

After you have checked the eight responses you most typically make to a disagreement, transfer both sets of
answers to the box on the next page by putting your intitial beside the words you chose.

AS SEEN FROM VIEWPOINT OF SELF:

:::::ATTITUDE TOWARD MY PARTNER:::::

	I value and affirm you.	*I do not value and affirm you.*
I do value and affirm myself.	DECLARE ["I messages"; I win and you win]	DEMAND ["you messages," fears; I win and you lose]
	2. negotiates 5. clarifies 8. explains 13. looks openly 20. compromises	4. forces 7. blames 9. criticizes 11. threatens 17. pressures
I do not value and affirm myself.	DEFER [too dependent; I lose and you win]	DEFECT [leaves partner; I lose and you lose]
	3. gives in 6. becomes silent 12. pretends 15. begrudges 18. surrenders	1. withdraws 10. evades 14. retreats 16. leaves room 19. disappears

:::::ATTITUDE TOWARD MYSELF:::::

Consider the box in which you each have the most answers. This may suggest that this style of dealing with conflict is the attitude you typically use with your partner. Consider how your own style relates to the style your partner shows in this exercise. Your answers may cluster in more than one box. Discuss some examples of the way each of you shows your approach to disagreements. Which attitude and style do you each perfer? Talk about any changes you would like to make in the way you handle your conflicts. (This exercise is based upon concepts presented by Narcisco and Burkett.)

Sometimes in conflict situations, partners respond in "get my way" behaviors. Some of these behaviors may be thought of as habits or typical emotional reactions. However, a closer look suggests that they are used by an individual to manipulate his or her partner. The partner who uses "get my way" behaviors is seeking to control the other in some way. Often both partners may be playing these types of games at the same time.

Some "get my way" behaviors are pouting, crying, blaming someone else, and pretending to be helpless or shy. Some shout or swear in efforts to control their partners. In the extreme, one partner may strike or cause physical pain to the other.

You may benefit by returning to the previous EXPLORE exercise and talking about the behaviors you each use when you are attempting to control or to get your way. Even a statement such as "If you loved me, you would . . . " can be an effort to control your partner.

You Define the Problem

Problems do not "just happen." On the contrary, a situation occurs, and in response to it, you and your partner decide whether it is a problem for either or both of you. Not all disagreements need to become problems. When you allow yourselves room to disagree and still to be accepted without losing face, then many conflicts can be resolved quickly.

Conflicts as Problems

A conflict exists when you try to do two or more things when it is possible to do only one. Conflicts also arise when one of you tries to do something that would prevent the other from carrying out a desired action. As a couple, you may have conflicts with others, such as relatives or friends. A conflict becomes a problem when you do not like what currently is happening, and you decide that the situation must be changed in some way.

Crisis as a Problem

A crisis is that point at which things seem to be happening faster than you can respond with the resources you have. A high level of stress is one sign of a crisis. Typically, a crisis implies that several troublesome events have happened to you in a short span of time. In a sense, the additional problem in a crisis may be that you cannot cope with the problems you already seem to have. You can see a crisis as a disaster that will destroy you, or you can use a crisis as an opportunity to grow through learning new ways to deal with problems.

Stress and Fatigue

Conflicts, crises, and problems increase your level of stress and the resulting fatigue. It is helpful to think of yourself as a system, composed of several physiological and psychological subunits. As an individual system, your best level of daily functioning occurs when all your subunits are working well together. As a couple, you and your partner combine your two individual systems into a "couple system." At the same time, you each continue to be a part of other systems, such as your work associates, circles of friends, families, and community.

When all is going well, all these systems are functioning at levels that best meet each individual's needs without hurting the other persons in the system. In part, working together in marriage is the creation of a two-person system that can meet the needs of both partners, while allowing each to continue to be satisfied in other interpersonal systems.

Any Change Causes Some Stress in the System

Changes at any point in a system may produce unexpected changes at other points in the individual or in the couple. Changes such as disagreements, conflicts, and unexpected events put more stress than usual on your marriage system. For most persons, unexpected change, whether good or bad, is stressful.

A couple or a family system works very much like an individual system. As an individual, your bodily systems have adapted to a typical, or normal, level of stimulation and stress. Too little stress allows the system to degenerate or "rust out," but too much stress overworks the system, causing it to break down or wear out faster than it can be rebuilt, or renourished. Too little excitement tends to produce boredom, listlessness, and feelings of rejection,

while too much stress produces anxiety, worry, frustration, and fatigue. Both extremes may lead to a loss of confidence and dissatisfaction.

Three Stages of Stress

1. *Alarm and awareness.* There are three basic stages in an individual's reaction to increased stress (Selye). Similar stages may occur in a two-person system (a couple). In the first stage, stress on an individual (or a couple) produces an initial alarm reaction. Changes in feelings and behaviors call attention to the problem and may result in increased alertness, greater sensitivity, muscle tension, and other reactions that are needed to cope with what may be a possible threat to the system.

2. *Resistance and coping.* In the second stage, action is taken to modify the events that are causing stress. Here the individual (or the couple) draws on skills and resources to correct the situation. If this action is successful, the system returns to its normal level of operation.

When the coping behaviors of the second stage are satisfactory, the stress is resolved and assimilated into the system. This brings the individual (or couple) a sense of relief, confidence, and success. Energy then can be renewed through relaxation and rest, and the full strength of the individual (or couple) is ready for other activities or the next stress.

3. *Exhaustion and defeat.* If the coping behaviors of stage two are not sufficient to overcome the stress, fatigue increases, a sense of frustration, anxiety, and inadequacy develops, and this may produce additional secondary stress. If a new stress occurs while the person (or couple) is in this third stage, it will add greatly to the feeling of being overwhelmed. Sometimes fatigue produces illness, and this may have the side benefit of removing the person from the initial stressful situation. Failure or illness also may bring the person (or couple) to others who can help to mobilize more resources to cope with the stress.

Explore: Stress Responses

Allow some time for you and your partner to review some of the recent changes you have had in your lives. Talk about how stressful each change was, or is, and the way you each responded to it. What specific actions did you take to cope with the stress?

A wedding can be quite stressful. If you and your partner are anticipating your wedding, discuss the changes related to it. What factors might present problems for you?

Consider the possible changes you may face in the next few weeks or months. Which changes, such as job or moving, might be most stressful? How will you cope with those stresses? Which pleasant, desirable changes also might be stressful for you?

Steps in Problem Solving

You and your partner will create your own marriage life-style, and it will include disagreements, heated arguments, conflicts, and differences of opinion. An event becomes a problem when either or both of you desire to change the outcome in some way.

To resolve a problem, you and your partner can take these basic steps. At the end of this section is an EXPLORE exercise that may be used to apply these steps to your own situation.

Agree on Time and Place to Discuss Problems

Before you actually work on the problem itself, you need to agree on the ground rules, or contract, to guide your problem solving. It is important to find a time that allows uninterrupted discussion of the issue, with only you and your partner present. It should not be when either of you is rushed or when something else requires your attention.

Another guide is to agree clearly on which problem you will consider, how long you will discuss it, whether anyone else should be present, and any other rules you feel necessary. For example, a good problem-solving contract might be stated in this way:

> We agree that after dinner tomorrow evening, we will decide which trip to make over the long weekend that we will have. No one else will be in on the discussion, and we will talk about it for not more than an hour, here at our place.

You also may agree that neither partner will mention the problem before the time you have set to discuss it. The remaining steps assume that you now have arrived at the time, place, and setting in which you actually will focus on the problem.

State the Problem Clearly in a Way That Is Agreeable to Both of You

To begin problem solving, be sure that both partners are discussing the same issue. Be very specific, letting each partner reflect his or her understanding of the problem and its details. Start by describing the actual event in question. To check

yourselves, you might pretend that you are taking pictures of the problem situation, so that all you can see is the behavior of each person involved. After the behaviors are clear, then allow more time to describe the interpretations, feelings, and intentions of each partner, in relation to the behavior. Be very careful to state any inferences about your partner as being the way you see the situation, not as facts. Here are some contrasting statements:

NOT THIS:

You don't love me like you used to. (too general)

You're not going to like this. (self-fulfilling prediction of failure)

You don't want me to have any fun. (mind reading)

MORE HELPFUL:

When you yelled at me last night, I felt angry and frightened, because I thought you did not like me. (states specific time and behavior and your feeling about it)

I would like to please you, but I feel so uncomfortable with your parents' criticism of us. (describes inner conflict about a proposed action)

It is very important to state the concrete, specific ways in which a situation or behavior creates a problem for you. To the other person, that behavior may not seem to be a problem. For example, if you do not like a certain type of clothes your partner wears, state the specific way this hurts you. It is not enough just to say, "I don't like it." It is essential that each of you states the way the behavior directly affects you.

Stating the problem clearly includes indicating which person has the problem. Each of you has many behaviors. Some of these are a problem for you, but not for your partner; some may be a problem for your partner, but not for you; and some may be a problem for both. Sometimes the same behavior may present a different problem for each partner.

Try to deal with only one problem at a time. Don't be surprised if one clearly stated problem seems to lead to other problems. Acknowledge the other problems, but continue to work on the issue you agreed to discuss. Hold the other issues for other problem-solving sessions.

State Your Present Reactions to the Problem

In stating the problem clearly, you included your feelings, interpretations, and intentions. Usually, you also have some feelings about having the problem, in addition to whatever feelings you had in the original problem situation itself. In other words, the problem affects you now in some definite way.

In the illustration given in Step 2, the person may have felt "angry and frightened" as part of the original problem. In addition, that person now may feel guilty about having those feelings or may be hesitant to talk about the event. In the situation concerning contact with parents, the partner may want to maintain a good relationship with the relatives and yet avoid unpleasant or unnecessary criticism.

These secondary feelings, which usually result from your sense of self-worth—your ego—can alert you to hidden investments you may have in the outcome of the problem. If you do not identify those investments clearly, you may choose a solution in order to prove you are "right," rather than choosing one to solve the original problem. If you can determine your self-investment, then you can consider it, also, as you develop a solution. This enables you to focus upon the full range of needs that you each have as persons.

State Your Objectives Clearly

As you consider the problem, state a specific request for the desired change. Identify, also, the person you think needs to make the change. Give your specific opinion about an outcome that would be better for you and for others involved. Compare these objectives:

NOT THIS:
I want things to be better. (not specific)
You must never do that again. (a demand)

MORE HELPFUL:
I'd like for our lovemaking to be more relaxed, with more patience from you, at a slower pace. (specifies goal)
I want us to be able to save at least 5 percent of our income this year. (states long-range goal)

Each partner needs an opportunity to state both the problem and the objectives as she or he sees the situation. These statements need to be clear enough so that each partner can easily state the other's perspective. You may not agree with your partner, but you can summarize what you hear him or her saying.

Consider Carefully All the Possible Alternate Solutions and Your Resources for Applying Them

After you agree on the problem, state your reactions to it, and agree on objectives, you can "brainstorm" possible solutions. In this step, don't worry about whether your ideas are practical or exactly right. It is usually helpful to take notes or to have some other way to keep up with possible answers. By developing several possible alternative actions, you can select the one that seems best, rather than taking the first one that comes to mind.

Together, you can evaluate your list of solutions in light of your goals, values, and standards. You may use a values-clarification procedure, such as ranking your responses according to the way they fit your moral standards. The end result does not justify the means, for the way you solve a problem is just as important as the result.

In most problem situations, you already have some resources for a solution. Your attitudes are important, and you and your partner are valuable resources, yourselves. Look for your inner beauty and possibilities. This is more significant than it may seem. In addition, either partner may possess the knowledge or skills that the solution requires.

Sometimes you may need to seek new information or assistance from reliable sources. Either or both of you may ask for help from others and listen to their suggestions and insights, but do not feel that you must follow their advice or suggestions. However, in some areas involving others, such as money management, property, or employment, good information about what legally can be done, or about the possible results of alternate actions, can aid you greatly in choosing a solution.

In deciding with whom to talk about alternatives, it is best to choose a trusted friend, minister, or professional person who is not directly involved in the problem in any way, since that would leave you and your partner free to make your own decisions.

Choose Your Plan and Carry It Out

In solving any problem, the time comes when you must act. You cannot choose not to choose, nor can you choose not to act. Even if you postpone a change in your actions indefinitely, that is a choice; although it may be a solution with results that are worse than the problem.

You probably never will have all the information and resources you would like, in order to find a guaranteed answer to your problem. Nevertheless, out of the possible solutions you and your partner have discussed, select one and actually implement it.

Your action plan may require changing the way you speak to your partner, rearranging your schedules, or taking a different view of the situation in order to make it less disturbing. It should give you as much control as possible over the outcome. The success of your solution will depend upon how well you and your partner carry out the parts of your plan.

Evaluate the Outcome of Your Actions

When you check the results of the action you took to resolve the problem, you will gain feedback about the changes you made. This is helpful for two reasons. If you achieved the goal you set as a solution, you will be able to reserve your plan as a possible strategy when a similar problem arises in the future. If your action did not resolve the problem, then you can check to discover the reasons, return to Step 1 to reformulate the problem more precisely, and be better informed as to the reason your action did not work.

Often a solution only partially achieves the objectives you set in Step 3. By looking at the plan and the results in detail, you and your partner can identify which actions helped, and which were not effective in reaching your goals. You can then continue the effective actions and agree on additional problem-solving sessions to improve other parts of your original plan.

Openness and Respect

Throughout the problem-solving process, it is essential to respect each other's feelings and opinions and to accept honest differences in views. Some differences are expected in any relationship. A 100 percent agreement on everything in a marriage may be a sign that one partner is too dominant and that the other is afraid to disagree. Seek to understand each other and to allow for individual views about facets of each problem.

The first time you use this problem-solving process, you may feel awkward or self-conscious. This is normal and to be expected. The procedure may seem mechanical or cold to some, but most couples who develop this type of problem-solving technique find that it works very well.

The results of this approach are well worth the investment of your time and energy. If you try to work through each problem when it is first noticed, you will prevent a buildup of the unresolved feelings and habits that lead to resentment and separation. In addition, successful problem solving builds love and increases your confidence in yourselves and in your relationship.

Explore: Problem Solving

With your partner, think about some recent conflict, disagreement, or crisis that was a problem for one or both of you. Use the seven steps we have listed to develop a plan; then apply the plan to the problem. These seven questions reflect the seven steps:

1. *Which problem do you agree to discuss, when, and where?*
2. *Have you stated the problem briefly and clearly by describing specific behaviors, feelings, interpretations, and expectations?*
3. *What are your current reactions to the problems?*
4. *What objectives would you like to accomplish? Do you agree on these?*
5. *What alternate solutions have you outlined?*
6. *Which solution will you use? Who will do which parts? How? When?*
7. *What happened as a result of your action? What are the next steps you need or want to take?*

Encourage and embrace each other at times, and describe your own feelings during the process.

When Your Procedure Does Not Work

If you and your partner fail to find a satisfactory solution to some problem, after you honestly have attempted to follow these problem-solving steps, you still have some alternatives. You may consult with your pastor, seek professional counseling, marriage therapy, financial consultation, or legal assistance. One good indication of your potential for growth is that you can agree to find help when you need it.

Marriage Counseling

Seeking personal or marital counseling actually involves the first five steps of the problem-solving procedure. You and your partner agree to discuss the problem (Step 1). In Step 2, you may state your problem as "We can't agree on the problem," or "Our problem is not knowing what the problem is." You may identify your reactions in Step 3 as being discouraged or worried about your relationship. The objective you find in Step 4 may be to stay together or it may be to find more satisfying lives separately. The alternative solution developed in Step 5 might be to see your minister or other professional counselor.

A marriage therapist may be a pastoral counselor, psychologist, social worker, psychiatrist, or other professional person, depending on the laws of your state. With your counselor, you and your partner can explore your situation more thoroughly and then implement the solution that you choose.

How do you know when you need professional

advice? If you are clear about the general type of assistance you need, seek a competent professional person in that field. If you are not, consult with your minister, your physician, or with a marriage and family therapist. Some sources for help are listed in the resources at the end of this book.

You Know You Need Professional Help When . . .

1. The attempt to solve problems produces more problems than solutions.
2. Something always seems to frustrate your solution.
3. You feel just as bad when the solution works as when it does not.
4. You never seem to find time to talk about problems.
5. One or both of you refuse to work on problems.
6. Most changes in your behavior are worse, not better.
7. You are certain you are okay; it is your partner who needs help.
8. You continue to feel depressed, no matter what your partner does or does not do.
9. You lose control of yourself in some situations. Examples: physical or verbal violence against your partner, abuse of medications or alcoholic beverages, compulsive behavior.
10. You hate to go home, or you wish your partner would not come home.
11. Fewer and fewer things seem to make sense.
12. You suspect your partner or others of wanting to harm you whenever they get the chance.
13. Most things seem to be beyond your control.
14. You feel guilty about most things, or you often feel you are a complete failure.
15. You can't define the problem and talking about problems only makes them worse.

If you answered yes to more than two or three of those statements, you and your partner probably should talk with your pastor or other counselor. It is best if you go as a couple, but it is better to seek help alone than not at all. If you are not sure whether to ask for help, go ahead, if only to clarify the way you are coping with your problems.

A Change of Focus

The first five chapters have considered some basic dimensions of your relationship. The resources, skills, and attitudes you have explored in those chapters are involved in all areas of your marriage. With this increased awareness of your backgrounds, process of communication, problem solving, and expectations, in the next four chapters we will turn to some specific issues in marriage.

Chapter 6

Uncovering Our Sexuality

There are many ways to love . . .
  and sex is one of them.
There are many sexual expressions of love . . .
  and sexual intercourse is one of them.

Through your sexual activities, you express your tenderness, care, and love for each other. Words of endearment, touches, smiles, and hugs are only a few of the expressions of your sexual love. As with other ways of communicating, sexual activities have a great deal of potential for providing shared meanings between partners. Occasions of physical and emotional closeness enable you to renew and deepen the love and grace that God offers you as a sexual being.

Sexuality is much more than nudity and genital contact between partners. Sexuality, as used here, includes all the ways that you express yourself—your personality—through your gender as female or male. Your thoughts, expectations, feelings, and wishes become known to your partner through the erotic possibilities that your body provides. Depending upon the way you feel about yourself and about your partner, your sexual behaviors can greatly enrich your intimacies as a couple.

Knowing Each Other

It is significant that the Bible uses the verb "to know" in describing sexual relations between a man and a woman. As you and your partner consider your feelings and wants concerning money, possessions, careers, friends, children, and other areas, you experience greater intimacy and closeness. Emotional closeness usually is expressed by being physically close enough to talk and to touch. This proximity makes your feelings, both positive and negative, more intense, partly because physical contact can bring either pain or pleasure. Thus your

sexuality is an important part of your intimacy and covenant as partners. Through your sexual relationship, you come to know each other more completely, and your unconditional acceptance of each other can become very real and beautiful.

Through sexual activity, your language of love inspires new creative forms, techniques, and approaches. Together, your sexual communication can be a growing crescendo of love as you freely and fully give yourselves to each other, with the deeper meanings of sexual love becoming most genuine through your long-term relationship.

More Than Information

Information about sexuality and sexual functioning is necessary for a happy and fulfilling relationship. However, your attitudes, values, warmth, respect, and tenderness with each other in lovemaking are much more important than sexual techniques and information. You can learn together and blend your skills into your own symphony of enjoyment. Like music and other forms of art, your sexual relationship depends upon the use of your mastery of basics to create more messages of love between your partner and yourself.

Some Basic Assumptions

Here are some Christian perspectives that express views about sexuality. As you read them, consider your own feelings and beliefs about your sexuality as a couple.

1. Your personality is expressed in dimensions that are both physical and spiritual. No action is only physical or only spiritual. For example, your personality and spirit are blended with body and brain to shape your thoughts into the words you

speak. Like all life, sex is both physical and spiritual—both flesh and spirit.

Since sexual behavior does have spiritual, emotional, intentional, and physical dimensions, you are not merely a sex organ, but a whole person. God has created you so that you can express yourself through your sexuality. Thus physical sex alone becomes an idol. God has created sex to be part of your whole lives together.

2. In the Bible and in current Christian thinking, human sexuality is clearly affirmed for its creative possibilities between partners. In the Old Testament, the Song of Solomon describes a wide range of sexual feelings as expressions of love between a man and a woman.

> How fair and pleasant you are,
>   O loved one, delectable maiden!
> You are stately as a palm tree,
>   and your breasts are like its clusters. . . .
> I am my beloved's,
>   and his desire is for me.
> Come, my beloved,
>   let us go forth into the fields . . .
> There I will give you my love. . . .
> The voice of my beloved!
>   Behold, he comes. . . .
> Let me see your face,
> for your voice is sweet,
>   and your face comely.
>   Song of Solomon,
>   7:6-7, 10, 12; 2:8, 14 (RSV)

With or without intercourse, sexual activities are affirmed by God and by the church today as major ways in which marriage partners can share love and tenderness and enrich each other as persons.

3. Women and men are equal before God in their participation in sexual expressions of love. Today some may consider the apostle Paul's comments about sexuality to be limited. However, in the context of New Testament life, his comments about married love were very advanced. For example, in I Corinthians, Paul assumed that a couple would have a full range of sexual relationships that could be initiated by either spouse. "Do not cheat each other of normal sexual intercourse, unless of course you both decide to abstain temporarily to make special opportunity for prayer. But afterwards you should resume relations as before" (I Cor. 7:5 Phillips).

4. On the basis of their covenant, partners choose together how they will express affection toward each other. It is important for both spouses that sexual preferences and concerns be discussed. When additional information is needed about any area of sexual functioning, partners can seek help together.

5. Sexual intercourse is for pleasure and procreation. Planning for the conception, birth, and parenting of children is the responsibility of both husband and wife. To assume this responsibility, both partners need accurate infomation about contraceptives in order to find a method for regular use that both prefer. Each child should be both wanted and planned.

6. A couple's understanding and agreement concerning sexual activities must be rooted in their response to God's covenant with them. Fidelity and faithfulness between partners refers to all areas of marriage, not just to sexual concerns. Faithfulness suggests that you and your partner can depend upon each other's love and care at all times. To be present, open, and concerned about each other expresses faithfulness and dependability between partners.

Explore: Sexuality

For this exercise, you will need magazines that contain pictures of adults of various ages. With your partner, select several pictures that you consider to be most expressive of the way you understand sexuality and intimacy between a man and a woman. Describe the way each picture shows this. Look also at other pictures that present distorted or misleading views of human sexuality. Give details for your reasons. Pictures may be from stories, advertisements, cartoons, or other sources.

Separately, write several sentences that describe the way you understand sexualty in your relationship. Give specific examples of behaviors that are important to you. Talk together about your statements. Touch or hold each other as you talk.

The Human Sexual-Response Cycle

Touching, caressing, massaging, holding, kissing, stroking, and hugging are some of the ways that you and your partner share joy and love. Loving talk, ways of dressing or undressing, smiles, and tone of voice convey important sexual meanings. This rich sexual vocabulary can express the feelings you have for each other, and may at times be a part of intercourse.

The human sexual-response cycle during intercourse has been described by Masters and Johnson as consisting of four major phases, each gradually progressing to the next level. Both men and women experience these four phases.

1. *Arousal and excitement.* Awareness of the pleasure of sexual contact with one's partner initiates this

stage. Arousal begins as one anticipates sexual intimacy. Tender caresses, strokes, kisses, and other foreplay activities increase sexual interest and prepare for intercourse. Perfume, music, and romantic talk add variety. Although these expressions of love are enjoyable in themselves, they are essential for adequate lubrication of the woman's vaginal area and for the man's penile erection.

2. *Plateau or leveling.* In this phase, sexual arousal continues for an extended time as partners continue to stimulate each other in mutually pleasurable ways. Learning additional ways to give and receive sexual pleasure helps partners to continue at a high level of arousal.

3. *Orgasm, or climax.* Orgasm occurs with a varied pattern of intense muscular contraction in both partners, including ejaculation by the male. On most occasions, partners will have orgasms at slightly different times. Several physiological reactions combine to produce intense pleasure for both partners. The intensity and pattern of orgasm in each partner depends upon energy levels, health, feelings, and attitudes.

4. *Resolution and relaxation.* During this fourth stage, there is a gradual return to the sexually nonexcited level. The fullness of personal sharing during this extended period of time can promote special closeness, unity, and renewal of appreciation between partners, bringing them together as more complete persons who know more of the mystery of each other.

Patterns Are Different

The sequence of excitement, plateau, orgasm, and resolution may or may not include coitus (penile-vaginal intercourse). Usually insertion of the penis into the vagina is part of the sequence, but the sexual-response cycle also may occur in relation to noncoital stimulation between partners. On some occasions partners may return to earlier excitement and additional orgasm experiences after relaxation and rest. A couples' patterns, levels, duration, intensities, and enjoyment of each stage will vary on different occasions of sexual activity; perhaps no two occasions will be identical.

Sexual interest, desire, and energy vary in each partner at different times and under different conditions. General health, fatigue, stress and tension, conflicts, menstruation, time schedules, moods, use of alcohol or other drugs, and other factors influence each partner's sensitivity. Some occasions of sexual activity end in disappointment or

frustration for every couple. From these, partners learn to appreciate and accept each other in new ways that can remove the pressure to perform perfectly in sexual areas.

Many times sexual intercourse and pleasuring will produce extreme ecstasy and a tremendous sense of oneness and mutual satisfaction. On other occasions they will be very comfortable and satisfying, without being prolonged or unusual. No one outcome is "correct," but every pattern and experience can be an opportunity to love and affirm each other through sexual relations.

Success In Sexual Relations

You and your partner are the only judges of your sexual compatibility and success. There is no criterion other than your own views and feelings. If you and your partner both are comfortable and pleased with your sexual behaviors, you are successful. The basic limit in the sexual area, as well as in all other areas, is that behaviors do not cause physical or emotional harm to either partner.

Sex is a matter of your entire mind and spirit, as well as a function of your genitals and the other parts of your body. Expectations, feelings, wants, and meanings are more important than physical factors in determining your sexual satisfaction and happiness. Since neither of you is a mind reader, it is essential that you continue to talk with each other about what is sexually satisfying for each of you. This open discussion helps to keep you aware of changes in your expectations and pleasurable behaviors.

Explore: Sexual Pleasuring

Talking about sexual preferences and behaviors may be more difficult than performing them. Allow some uninterrupted private time together to share your feelings about discussing sexual matters. You might begin by completing this sentence: "When I talk about sex, I feel . . ."

When you become more comfortable, consider some of the sexual activities you enjoy, or would enjoy. Describe the behavior, tell what it means to you, and talk about how you feel. What expectations about sexual intimacy does each of you bring to your marriage? Which behaviors do you dislike? At which times do you feel rejected or most loved by what your partner wants or does?

Sexual Difficulties

Some sexual difficulties occasionally occur for most couples. Many times the difficulty will disappear if the partners do not become upset, anxious, demanding, or preoccupied with the problem. Incorrect or limited information about sexual functioning may cause problems for partners. Partners often can increase their sexual satisfaction by obtaining good sexual information and training. Some resources listed in this book can provide additional information.

There are several common sexual dysfunctions which typically have psychological causes:

IN MALES:

Erectile dysfunction—inability to achieve and/or maintain erection sufficient to complete coitus, on an average of at least three-fourths of the occasions of intercourse.

Premature ejaculation—ejaculation occurs too soon, usually within less than a minute after entry into the vagina.

Ejaculatory incompetence—inability to ejaculate inside the vagina, but ejaculation may result from masturbation.

IN FEMALES:

Orgasmic dysfunction—either never has had an orgasm or has had orgasms previously but not at present.

Dyspareunia—painful intercourse, even with sufficient foreplay and vaginal lubrication.

Vaginismus—powerful, painful involuntary contraction of vaginal muscles which prevents entry of penis.

If a sexual difficulty or dysfunction continues to prevent satisfactory sexual relations, you and your partner can seek appropriate professional assistance. Your minister or physician can help you to clarify the issues and locate well-qualified professional persons, if needed.

Some techniques for overcoming sexual difficulties are simple to use and are described in McCary, in Masters and Johnson, and in other sources. Often sexual difficulties reflect other areas of the partners' relationship. Exploring the attitudes, values, preferences, self-images, expectations, and other factors presented in this guide also may help partners to more enjoyable sexual relations. Your covenant of unconditional love becomes especially important in this area.

Contraception

There are several adequate methods to control conception in the event a couple does not wish to conceive a child. These are listed under three headings below. You may obtain more details from the resources listed in this book, and your minister, counselor, or physician also can assist you. Some community agencies, such as Planned Parenthood and city or county health departments provide inexpensive assistance with contraceptives.

UNRELIABLE METHODS

These contraceptive methods are not dependable:

Douche—This is not necessary and often not recommended for feminine cleanliness. The douche cannot reach sperm that have entered the uterus.

Rhythm—Most women do not know the precise time of their ovulation until after it occurs—too late for contraceptive action.

Withdrawal—Concentrated quantities of semen often are contained in the fluid that discharges from the penis prior to ejaculation, and as a result, semen may be deposited in the vagina before ejaculation occurs.

FAIRLY RELIABLE METHODS

These methods, if carefully used before intercourse, provide reasonably good contraception without a physician's prescription:

Condom—This must be of good quality and placed on the penis before it is inserted in the vagina; it is the only contraceptive that also protects against venereal disease.

Contraceptive cream, jelly, or foam—These can be effective, if carefully and properly inserted in the vagina early enough before intercouse.

Contraceptive cream and condom—Although considered more troublesome, this combination provides more reliable contraceptive protection than condom or cream alone.

PRESCRIPTION METHODS

These methods are usually the most reliable, and they require a physician's prescription or other assistance:

Oral contraceptives—"The pill" is safe and reliable only if used under the supervision of a physician. Some women have side effects from certain types of contraceptive medications. Some physicians advise being "off the pill" to check on body rhythms occasionally, usually for a period of several months every two or three years.

Intra-uterine device (IUD)—This consists of an inert material inserted into the woman's uterus by a physician. The IUD can be used successfully by some women, provided they have annual checkups by a physician.

Diaphragm and contraceptive jelly or cream—The diaphragm must be fitted for the woman by a physician, but it does not involve a chemical change in the woman's body, as produced by the pill, or long-term inserts, such as the IUD. It must be reinserted correctly into the vagina prior to each intercourse.

Permanent sterilization surgical procedures (vasectomy for the man, usually tubal ligation for the woman)—These methods are considered permanent and are done only at a time when a couple is certain they never wish to conceive children.

Newer contraceptive methods currently are being tested. To secure more information about them, consult with specialists in your community.

Physical Examinations for Both Partners

If you have not done so recently, it is helpful for each of you to have a physical examination. At that time, you can consult with your physician about any sexual and contraceptive concerns you may have. If you have a physical condition that might affect your participation in sexual activities, or if you have concerns about inheritable genetic factors that might affect any children you conceive, talking with specialists in these areas can give you important information and often relieve you of unnecessary worries.

Couple Sexuality

You and your partner determine your sexual activities, as part of your total relationship as a couple. Often your sexual expressions reflect what is happening in other areas of your marriage. Your pleasurable sexual relationship can increase your appreciation of each other and add to those other areas.

We want to emphasize that it is very important that you and your partner continue to talk openly and frankly with each other about your sexual values, patterns, concerns, and desires. Sexual matters sometimes are difficult or embarrassing for couples to discuss because so much personal self-worth may be invested in sexuality. However, acknowledging these feelings together can help you to be more comfortable with the beautiful, God-given expressions of your sexual love.

Explore: Issues in Sexuality

Take enough uninterrupted time together to talk about the information and issues presented here. These questions are worth discussing. Add other topics that are important for you.

1. *What do you like, and dislike, about being a woman/man? Can you remember when you first became aware of yourself as a girl/boy? How would you feel if you were the opposite sex?*

2. *What sex education did you receive from your mother, father, relatives, other adults, and friends your own age? What attitudes that developed from these experiences are still with you now?*

3. *Do you have any physical condition that may affect sexual relations with your partner? If so, discuss with your partner information and suggestions about ways you can enjoy sexual intimacy in the context of your physical limitations.*

4. *What emotional or psychological characteristics do you think are more typical of men, or of women? Talk about these together.*

5. *When do you feel most "sexy" and attractive to your partner? When is your partner most sexually attractive to you? When are you most sexually excitable? . . . least excitable or interested in sex? What "turns you on" or "turns you off" sexually? How do physical and emotional rhythms affect you sexually?*

6. *Which five words best describe sexual activities? Separately, write at least five words, including slang terms, to describe sexual activities. Then compare these together. Which words express hostility or control of the partner? Which words emphasize love and thoughtfulness for the partner?*

7. *Sometimes feelings of affection and appreciation for other persons (of both the same and the opposite sex) may be confused with heterosexual or homosexual tendencies. Some persons may have experienced sexual abuse, rape, or homosexual advances. Talk about your feelings concerning these areas.*

8. *How do you express your sexual identity as a person, through your dress, speech, gestures, behaviors, and other ways? Describe some of these and talk about the meanings they have for you both.*

9. *What type of contraceptive method will, or do, you use in your marriage? Whose decision is this? Do you each feel equally responsible for contraception? Some couples conceive much more easily than others, but usually this cannot be known until a couple attempts to have a child. The safest approach is to assume that you might become pregnant with every intercourse and to use contraceptives accordingly.*

10. *What would you do if you had an unwanted pregnancy? How does each of you feel about abortion?*

11. *If you do not already have children, do you plan to allow yourselves at least a year or two to adjust to each other in marriage before you conceive a child?*

12. *What concerns do you have about venereal disease in relation to your sexual activities together?*

Now for the Symphony

With patience and gentleness, explore your sexuality together, being guided by your own awareness of the activities that are uplifting, enjoyable, and stimulating. Freedom, variety, and pleasant surprises can add to your sexual joy, and this will expand into other areas of your relationship. There will be times when sex is not exciting or ecstatic, but together, you can accept those times and learn from them. Your growth occurs as you come to appreciate your uniquenesses and your differences, blending these in your own ways in your artistic creations of your sexual love for each other.

Chapter 7

Money, Possessions, and Work

It's not what you would do
  If millions should be your lot,
It's what you are doing now
  With the fifteen dollars you've got!

The way you use your time, money, and belongings reveals your values. Although the grammar in the above rhyme could be improved, it emphasizes that money, possessions, and work are linked together in both practical and emotional ways for each person. Your use of money shows the way you trade your work and resources for the work and resources of others, and your belongings are the accumulation of this process. In these ways you and your partner express your covenant with each other and your stewardship of your part of God's Creation.

God calls each of us to service in the world. Whether paid or volunteer, your work can be your response to God's call to you to minister and care for others. Your Christian stewardship is based upon your belief that ultimately the world and everything in it belongs to God, who loans it to us for our use.

Money

The handling of your money involves two major functions. These are (a) the executive-decision tasks and (b) the secretary-treasurer tasks. You can arrange your spending in many different ways. Maintaining good credit relieves anxiety and shows your responsibility as a couple. Your handling of finances can enhance your relationship, or it can strain and perhaps destroy it.

1. In *the executive-decision tasks*, you and your partner need to agree on the way you will make decisions concerning the use of your money. You may determine that in certain categories, one of you will implement the decisions, as with buying groceries or gasoline. In other purchases, such as home furnishings or a car, you may decide that both partners must be fully involved.

2. The jobs called *the secretary-treasurer tasks* include balancing your checkbook, paying bills, writing checks, and keeping good records of income and expenditures. In deciding which partner will do each of these, you will need to consider which of you has more time, skill, and interest in each job. It can be either husband or wife, providing you agree on the general procedure.

Be clear in separating the secretary-treasurer from the executive-decision functions. Sometimes it is easy to assume that the person who writes the checks automatically has final say over the way money is spent. Prompt payment of obligations and good record-keeping require the cooperation of both partners. This helps to eliminate many arguments over "where the money has gone."

It helps to have a regular time each week or month to discuss details of your income and spending. This also can be a time to renew goals and discuss longer-range expenditures and larger purchases.

On Giving Away Money

One way to express your appreciation for the blessings you receive through work and money is to share these resources. Setting aside a specific percentage of your income (a tithe) to assist others is a helpful way to share. Many times, 10 percent of a couple's total income can be set aside for the church and for community and world needs. This can become a lifelong pattern of generous sharing, and for this reason, it is placed near the top of the budget outline that follows. Giving to others is so important in helping couples regard the use of all their income as a stewardship of God's resources.

Explore: Managing Your Money

In this exercise, you can explore your basic plans for managing your money. Allow plenty of time to discuss your executive-decision tasks first. In your relationship now, who decides how money will be spent? Which items are mutual decisions, and which does each partner make separately? How do you both feel about your decision patterns?

In your marriage, will you (or do you) have a joint checking account, separate accounts, and/or credit cards? Will you pool your incomes, or keep them identifiably separate? How do you feel about your method of paying for purchases? Are there times when either of you tries to use money to control your partner? Which of the secretary-treasurer tasks will each of you do?

After you have talked about your money-management functions, plan additional time to set up your income and spending plan. Whether you call this a budget, a plan, or something else, it still means that you and your partner are the ones who decide how much money will be set aside for each category.

You may make your entries independently and then combine them in this chart, or you can each place a figure on the line as you talk together about each category. With either procedure, be alert to your feelings as you arrive at your figures.

Begin by assuming a realistic amount for your income for the next twelve months.

Our Annual Income:
$_____ *from wife's work, career, job*
$_____ *from husband's work, career, job*
$_____ *from other sources*
$_____ Total Annual Income

Divide the total by 12 to find your
Monthly Average Income: $_____
If your income varies during the year, finding your monthly average can help you plan to hold extra income from the higher months to use in the low-income months.

You may prefer to subtract your taxes and Social Security payments to arrive at your
Monthly Take-Home Income: $_____

Your Spending Plan:	Initial Amounts		Adjusted Amount	Actual Amounts (if available)
	HUSBAND	WIFE		
taxes and Social Security	____	____	____	____
emergencies	____	____	____	____
health, life insurance	____	____	____	____
contributions: church, others	____	____	____	____
housing, utilities	____	____	____	____
food (including eating out)	____	____	____	____
clothing	____	____	____	____
personal money for wife	____	____	____	____
personal money for husband	____	____	____	____
transportation expenses, payments, and maintenance	____	____	____	____
payments for purchases on credit	____	____	____	____
leisure and recreation	____	____	____	____
job-related expenses	____	____	____	____
education	____	____	____	____
savings	____	____	____	____
other expenditures	____	____	____	____
TOTALS	$____	$____	$____	$____

Take time to talk about balancing your expenditures and income. Share together the way you feel about details of your money management.

Taxes and Social Security were included in the list on page 51 as a reminder of the part of your income that goes for those purposes.

Other Money Issues

Here are some additional concerns that many couples consider. Select the issues that are important for you and your partner and discuss them together.

1. Every married couple should have *wills* that are up to date, with terms that are agreeable to both partners. A will can avoid complicated probate court procedures in the event of the death of one partner. It may include many matters, such as guardianship of children, provision for care of family, tax implications, trusts, disability income, insurance, pensions, and property. In the case of a couple, a will usually names the surviving spouse as executor. You will need to consult with an attorney about details of your wills.

2. Some partners may have *property* that they would like to continue as legally separate after entering marriage. If you wish to maintain any possessions as legally belonging only to one partner, you will need to consult an attorney about details. State laws concerning property vary considerably. In addition, you and your partner need to share your feelings about these decisions. In some cases, maintaining separate property may be a way to protect the legal or personal interests of children of a previous marriage. It also may be a subtle expression of uncertainty or lack of trust in your relationship with your partner. In many situations, separate property arrangements are merely good business procedures.

3. If both partners are employed, *how much of both incomes must be used for your basic expenses?* It is important to talk about alternate plans in case of pregnancy, serious disease, or disabling injury. Changes in the economy may cause an unexpected loss of income from some jobs.

If you never have experienced living on your own income, you and your partner might take the amount set aside for food on your spending plan in the EXPLORE exercise, and go to a supermarket or other store to price items you would need for two weeks of meals. You also might shop for a major home appliance and compare the costs of paying cash with buying on credit.

4. For some couples, *credit installment payments and unpaid debts* are problems. Some persons may be impulse buyers, or they may have prewedding debts that must be paid after the wedding. It is essential to be honest about debts, loans, and other financial obligations that may become part of your marriage. Feelings about these matters need to be discussed openly, also.

5. If you plan to have children, what are the *options you might have for working after the baby arrives?* Some couples have decided that both partners will work part-time, so that each can share in the parenting. In many cases, both partners continue in their full-time jobs by using the services of a trusted, competent person, or agency, for child care.

6. Some partners have *previous financial obligations* to their children or to parents that will affect availability of money in the marriage. If you are involved with child-support payments, what adjustments need to be made in relation to your current partner? Is either partner financially responsible for parents or other relatives? Both plans and feelings about these obligations need to be discussed. Even if you are not involved now in these obligations, you and your partner might talk over your feelings and ideas about parents or other relatives who may become your financial responsibility in the future.

Times for Review

Income, expenditures, and other financial matters change during a marriage. It is important to have times when you and your partner can discuss comfortably all money and income issues. You also can find information and assistance in books, personal finance seminars, and from banks, insurance, and home finance companies. Financial opinions and advice vary widely, and you need to evaluate all information from the viewpoint of Christian stewardship in your marriage.

Space and Property

Your residence is more than just a place to eat, sleep, and store your belongings; it also reflects your interests and values. It is an extension of yourself. Damage to your residence by fire or theft is threatening both because of its financial cost and because of your emotional investment in your possessions. This emphasizes the fact that your home carries at least two levels of meaning for you and your partner.

1. Functional and practical use. Most items in your residence have a specific use. For example, chairs are for sitting and a refrigerator is for storing food. The practical use of furniture seldom is related to its style or price.

2. Emotional, psychological meaning. Your residence and furnishings also have emotional value for you. For instance, some pictures carry meanings and memories of persons important to you. The quality and style of furnishings, books, and other possessions may involve your feelings of self-worth. A certain furniture arrangement may be a matter of "getting your way," as much as for convenience.

Explore: Living Space

Allow time together to share your ideas and feelings about your residence and possessions. If possible, go to a residence that you have had, now have, or will have, as a couple.

1. *Consider together the current or recent residential situation (room, apartment, house, or other) of each partner. What three things did you like best? What were three disadvantages? Describe these.*
2. *Talk about the residential situation you will have, or hope to have.*
   a. *In which room will you probably spend most time? . . . least time?*
   b. *Who will be responsible for keeping each area clean and in order? How will the other partner help?*
   c. *How much closet, drawer, and storage space will you each need?*
   d. *Which area do you value most? . . . least? Describe your reasons.*
3. *What special hobbies, activities, and interests do you have that will require space in your home? How will you decide on this?*
4. *What other property, such as automobile, bicycles, and so on, do you have that will require storage? How will you arrange this?*
5. *Will you rent, lease, or buy your residence? What issues are involved in this decision?*
6. *How do you feel about moving to a new residence? How will you locate stores, professional services, and friends? What makes a residence feel like home to you?*
7. *Which jobs will each partner do to keep your residence clean, in good repair, and livable? If necessary, could either of you do any job around your residence, including cooking, washing dishes, fixing things, and cleaning?*
8. *How will you share in these decisions? What feelings do you each have as you think together about your residence? Talk more about these.*

Some Stewardship Concerns in Relation to Property

Our Christian commitment challenges us, as couples, not only to consider our own needs, resources, talents, and careers, but also to place ourselves in the context of God's world. Our Christian stewardship leads us to think about community, national, and world issues as we plan our family budgets and make decisions related to our vocations, possessions, and money.

Explore: Major Human Concerns

In the process of looking at important personal, couple, and family issues, it is easy to overlook some of the major concerns that face us all as part of the world community. You and your partner can take some time to talk about these and similar questions:

1. *How much of the world's energy do you use? How much of it is from nonrenewable sources, such as petroleum? How much of your residence and transportation energy comes from renewable sources, such as water or solar power?*
2. *What proportion of the world's resources are rightfully yours as a couple, if you are concerned about couples and families everywhere?*
3. *How do you feel about the overpopulation and intense hunger of persons in many areas of the world? What are you doing about these or other needs of other families?*
4. *What are your other community, national, or world concerns, as you and your partner consider your jobs, money, and possessions? In your responses to these concerns, what difference is made by a Christian stewardship view?*

Work, Job, Career, Vocation

As a Christian, you may interpret your work, whether paid or not, as being God's call to serve. Some persons feel that their calling is to use their skills and talents to meet the needs of the world. You are called to be a person for God.

Work has been so much a part of our nation's value-system that it is sometimes hard to see ourselves as valuable persons if we are not paid, or paid well enough, for our work. Persons who are too young, not physically able, too old, or who choose not to work for hire often have been made to feel that their contributions are unimportant or second class. An important step is to recognize these pressures when they appear and to accept ourselves fully, even though we do not have the power or ability to be a part of the well-paid work elite.

Some Dimensions of Work

There are at least six major dimensions involved in choosing or in changing your work and career. As you understand these dimensions more fully, you probably will consider your work more satisfying.

1. *Interests:* What do you enjoy doing? What about life excites you? What do you dislike? If you had the necessary training and education, what job would you choose? How much of your time and energy goes into your interests?
2. *Abilities:* What can you do well? Where have you succeeded or not done well? What are your work skills? What training do you have, or need?
3. *Goals:* What are your objectives in life? What would you like to have achieved five years from now? . . . twenty years from now?
4. *Expectations of Others:* What job or career do others want you to pursue? Must you conform to their expectations? How do they control your choices?
5. *Opportunities:* Will some business or other unit of society pay you to do what you want to do and can do? Can you create a paying job for yourself?
6. *Rewards:* What rewards or results are important to you? Is it most important to do something interesting, to achieve a certain goal, to make a lot of money, or to have job security? What rewards do you want? How will you know when you have received your rewards? How much money or other rewards will you require?

Explore: Meanings of Work

Take time with your partner to exchange feelings and attitudes toward yourselves and work. These guides may help:
1. *How does your job or occupation express the person you are? Does it mean more to you than just a way to earn money?*
2. *Together, consider Jesus' story of the three persons who had different talents (money or abilities), in Matthew 25:14-30. Talk also about the meaning of the statement, "Where your treasure is, there will your heart be also" (Matt. 6:21 RSV).*
3. *What do you do, paid or not paid, that gives you a sense of being valuable and worthwhile?*
4. *Share the way you feel when you cannot do the work you want to do. What if you cannot find satisfying work, or cannot find any job at all? How do you deal with disappointments and dissatisfaction in your work?*

Career Development Stages

Adults have developmental stages, just as do infants, children, and adolescents. Each year of your life will be different, as you can explore in chapter 10. Each year builds, in important ways, on previous experiences, and yet it offers new opportunities for creative choices and satisfying work, which you may be unable to see at the present time.

Across your lifetime, your jobs will change, the meaning you attach to your work will change, and the needs of society for certain types of work also will change. There are several ways to view these changes. An overview of your possible work stages can help you to become more intentional about the way your jobs relate to your marriage. If you make a major change, from one type of work or career to another, you may restart the cycle, depending on the similarity between your old work and your new.

Your view of your own life career-stages is influenced by several factors. The stages summarized here assume that the world of work and the world economy will remain comparatively stable. They also assume that individuals have access to necessary training and receive encouragement to develop appropriate work skills. Career stages also are affected by the increasing opportunities for people to set their own time agendas for paid work, family, and other involvements.

1. *Precareer Preparation:* This is the stage when trade school, college, professional, or other training is obtained, to prepare for entry-level positions in specific occupational areas.
2. *Entry:* In the first few years, a person is gaining experience. These job positions require minimum preparation and no experience. Job changes within a company, or from one company to another, may be from one beginning position to another.
3. *Establishment and Advancement:* During this period, a person is achieving promotions, gaining more status and authority in a line of work, and moving to a maximum level of competence and security. This stage usually takes place during a person's late twenties, and into the forties. For some who enter a career area later in life, these first three stages may be shortened because of experience gained in family or other areas.
4. *Maintenance or Reassessment:* On the basis of earlier achievements, in this period a person continues at a high level of work productivity, which often includes management responsibility, such as that of foreman or administrator, or the operation

of a self-owned business. Depending on the type work and the opportunities, this stage is typical of persons in their forties and fifties. For some, this is a time of disenchantment because of health, family changes, or perceived failures. Some persons may change to an entirely new career area, if opportunity and experience permit.

5. *Retirement or Reengagement:* Realistic assessment of one's individual work abilities and interests, retirement laws, and opportunities for continued work are important factors for employment in later life. While official retirement concludes work careers for many, continued employment or alternate occupations are options for others. Age alone does not determine a person's capability or a person's desire to work. For some, this is a period of greatest community and volunteer involvement and presents an opportunity for hobbies or travel.

The root word for vocation is "to call" or "to make vocal." Your vocation is one way to make your personality known in the world about you. It is your "calling." In a sense, you have at least three vocations, listed in the order of their relative importance.

1. You are obligated to become the best person that you can be. This is basic to marriage, work, and leisure.
2. Your marriage also is a calling—to create and to bring to reality some of the many opportunities that are possible with your partner.
3. The work through which you contribute to the world beyond self and family, for pay or as a volunteer, is a third vocation.

Explore: Work Issues

Take some relaxed time to talk with your partner about issues that are important to you and your relationship. You may want to make some notes independently and then come together to talk about them.

1. *What career does each of you plan? What do you imagine you will be doing, in ten or fifteen years?*
2. *For the husband: How do you feel about your wife's work? Will her career satisfy her? In what ways will you encourage your wife in her work and career goals?*
3. *For the wife: How do you feel about your husband's work? Will his career satisfy him? In what ways will you encourage your husband in his work and career goals?*
4. *How would you like your partner to feel about your work, both paid and volunteer? What problems and possibilities will the work of each partner present for your marriage?*
5. *Consider the way job factors such as hours, work schedules, travel, necessary clothes, work associates, opportunities, pay, location, and required moves to new communities may, affect your marriage. Is the job dangerous or tension-producing? Is it worthwhile to you? . . . to your partner? . . . to others?*
6. *What type of education is necessary for your careers? How does each partner feel about additional training that may be required or desirable?*
7. *How important is the income from your job, in comparison to the type work it is, your enjoyment of it, and its prestige? With your jobs, can you finance your marriage in the way you would like?*
8. *Will your job involve working with a parent, relative, or close friend? If so, what possible conflict might develop between you, your partner, and these other persons?*
9. *Under what circumstances would you change to a different job? Might this occur in the near future?*
10. *What crises might unexpectedly alter your career plans? Discuss these and the way you might prepare for them.*

Which Comes First?

Money, possessions, and jobs all are parts of your marriage, yet they are very personal aspects of your lives as individuals. They present potential problems, as well as opportunities for growth, because they usually force decisions about your relationship as a couple. If the amount of money you have available is limited, you may be able to carry out only some of the activities you have planned.

Money also is power, and decisions about money may involve shifts in the amount of power or control that each of you has in your relationship. These power issues also may appear in decisions about your residential space and the things you own.

Job requirements, especially, may raise power and priority issues for you and your partner. Advancement in your career field may require overtime and intensive work away from home. Your employer may expect you to give your job priority over your marriage, but you and your partner may want to place your relationship first. You may be forced to choose between marriage and job priorities, at times when it is difficult to make those decisions. It is essential to continue to talk with each other about these issues.

In the areas of money, possessions, and work, you

and your partner have limitless opportunities to apply your own viewpoints and commitments. Money itself is not the root of problems, but the value you place on money and possessions may cause difficulties (I Tim. 6:10). There is constant change in the way you blend your work, money, and marriage, and it must continue to be open to your discussion and negotiation of priorities. These are opportunities for you to grow in your relationship.

Chapter 8

Children and Others

. . . We are sometimes childlike, sometimes childish, but always, we are God's children.

. . . Marriage and parenthood are living parables which enable us to better understand God.

Your covenant with each other is the basic bond that holds you together, as partners in marriage. The quality of your relationship greatly affects the way you relate to your relatives and friends, and to your own children, if you choose to have them.

Children make a huge difference in marriage. It is up to you and your partner to decide whether you will have children and how you will relate to them. If you already have children, you continue to choose, every day, the way you will treat them. Your covenant as spouses is a major key to these decisions.

If you choose to conceive or adopt children, or if you already have children, your marriage and other relationships become more complicated. Each of you is both spouse to your partner and parent to your child or children. With any three persons, in times of conflict, it is tempting for two to take sides against the third person. When sharp triangles exist, it is difficult to maintain a happy family circle.

This is a positive opportunity for you and your partner to consider your children, and also others, as members of a cooperative team of persons who share mutual support. These persons can love and care for one another and work together for the good of all. This cooperation is not automatic, for it takes attitudes of love and respect to develop this caring community, in which a gain for one is a gain for all, and a sadness or loss for one affects all who are involved.

This covenantal perspective offers you support as you consider whether to have children and/or how best to parent the children you already may have. You provide important models for your children, yet you encourage them to absorb the good characteristics of others, as well. You affirm your children and other relatives, yet you know there are others who also care. It is a relief to realize that as a parent, you do not have to do everything alone. You are not the only emotional support for your children.

The fellowship of the Christian church helps you in your marriage and as parents. The Christian community, at its best, expresses this graceful relationship between persons, regardless of age, sex, status, or other characteristics. Within the context of the church as the household of God, your marriage and family can be the church in your home.

Alternatives Concerning Children

The attention you give to the following paragraphs depends upon the present situation of you and your partner, in relation to children in your marriage. Consider these possibilities and then explore those that apply to you.

1. We plan never to have children.
2. We plan to conceive or adopt children.
3. We are expecting a child.
4. We now have children and may plan more.

In each of these situations, there are special factors that affect the marriage relationship.

1. *Choosing not to become parents.* Not every couple will choose to become parents. We hope that every child will be a wanted child, although, unfortunately, some couples have parenthood thrust upon them. Couples may have good reasons for wanting to remain childless. Their careers may make parenthood difficult. Some partners may be involved in other helpful activities that are satisfying—perhaps working directly with other people's children. Some persons simply do not enjoy being with children or

adolescents. Because some parents, relatives, or friends expect a married couple to have children, it may be difficult for the couple to explain their nonparent status to others, and agreement on the explanations to others may be a necessary aspect of nonparenthood. It also is important that both partners continue to be comfortable with their decision.

Explore: Not Being Parents

If you and your partner do not want to become parents at any time in your marriage, discuss your feelings. Talk with other couples who have made the same decision. What factors might cause you to change your mind later, perhaps when you are too old to have children? When do you enjoy helping others' children? What past experiences, career motives, or other factors are involved in your decision? When, if ever, does either of you feel defensive about your nonparent status? How do you respond to those who expect you to have children?

2. *Children are in our future.* It usually is preferable for you and your partner to be alone for at least a year or two after your wedding, to allow you to adjust to each other before your children arrive. As discussed in chapter 6, proper use of appropriate contraceptives gives you control over the time children come into your lives.

There are many constructive reasons for wanting children. Partners who are secure with each other as spouses may desire to share this love and happiness. Parenting involves a willingness to devote many years to caring for children and helping them grow into maturity. Good parents treat their children as individuals with rights and dignity, and as they seek to understand their growing children, they also discover new insights about themselves. Parenting may be for you, if you enjoy children and like to play, work, and share with them.

Some couples may want children for poor reasons. A person who is lonely and hungry for love may want a child in order to receive affection. Some persons conceive children as a way to prove their sexual potency or to solve marriage problems. Children do not "hold a marriage together." On the contrary, parenthood tests the commitment of spouses to each other and to the children. In many ways, the presence of children in your home places additional strain on your relationship as partners.

No one can be a perfect parent, yet parenting is an investment in the future. If parents genuinely love their children and provide dependable care for them,

the children will discover this and respond in increasingly mature ways. One objective of parents is to work themselves out of their roles by enabling their children to become more independent and to enjoy life by themselves.

Explore: Planning to Become Parents

With your partner, share your dreams and feelings about being parents. Some of these questions may be important to consider:

1. *What are your reasons for wanting children?*
2. *What kinds of experiences with children have you had? Did you have younger brothers or sisters for whom you cared? How do you feel about your own family situations as they have involved children?*
3. *What do you hope, or fear, having children will be like?*
4. *What do you want most to do with, and/or for, your children?*
5. *How many children do you want? How many daughters and/or sons?*
6. *What if your child is severely limited or handicapped in some way? Does either of you have a genetic history which indicates that your children might inherit a disease or malformation? Have you carefully checked this possibility? Have you discussed it with appropriate medical experts? How do you feel about this?*
7. *Are you able to conceive children? If you and your partner could not conceive, what alternatives would you consider? Would you adopt children? Would you consider artificial insemination? If you never have conceived together, what if, perhaps after years of careful use of contraceptives, you discover that you cannot conceive? Discuss your feelings in these areas.*
8. *Suppose you have an unplanned pregnancy. How would this affect your other plans, such as changing jobs, moving, or completing additional education? Under what circumstances would you seek an abortion, if at all? What backup plans and resources do you have for this possibility?*

3. *Now pregnant.* Although it is the woman who becomes pregnant, a pregnancy continues, as well as begins, as a couple matter. You and your partner may have read and discussed the concerns mentioned in "Children Are in Our Future." Pregnancy is not a disease, and it can be an exciting time, with partners coming to appreciate each other in new ways. In addition, together with other expectant couples, spouses can participate in prenatal and childbirth classes. It is essential to secure adequate prenatal care as early as possible.

Although pregnancy is not an adequate reason for marriage, some couples may feel pressured for that reason. With a premarital pregnancy, it is essential for the couple to think about other alternatives, as well as marriage, with a minister or counselor. The issues and procedures in this book can be most helpful in this process.

Explore: Pregnancy

Talk with your partner about your feelings concerning pregnancy. If your pregnancy has been planned as part of your marriage, discuss the changes it brings. How will, or do, you support each other during pregnancy? What will you do if you have an unexpected or unplanned pregnancy? Share your feelings and some of the sources of these feelings.

4. *Now have children and may have more.* If you and/or your partner have children from a previous marriage, many additional factors are involved in your own marriage. For some partners, there are decisions about child support and visitation rights by the ex-spouse. Deciding with which parent the children will live is fundamental and sometimes difficult. There are also decisions about the new partner's adoption of his or her mate's children and about involvement in parenting. The parent's new spouse becomes, in many ways, an "instant parent."

If you have children from a previous marriage, and you plan to have more children with your current partner, the ages of the children sometimes may become a factor. Much depends upon how each partner feels about the present children, as compared to future children. When partners work together in helping children adjust to the new marriage, blended families can be just as successful as others. If parents tend to consider each child as "his" or "hers," then these underlying attitudes of fear and uncertainty may make adjustments more difficult.

Explore: Instant Parents and Blended Families

If you and/or your partner now have children, you probably have discussed and experienced the way they affect your relationship. As appropriate to your situation, consider these issues.

1. *Describe your feelings about each child. What changes has each made in your relationship?*

2. *If you are divorced and have children from your previous marriage, what changes in child support, visitation rights, and other areas will you make in relation to your current marriage? Discuss the feelings of your partner and your former spouse.*

3. *If you are widowed, talk about the way your adjustments relate to your partner now. What reactions do your children have to your new marriage?*

4. *How do your children feel about having a "new" mother or father? In your current relationship, how will you, your partner, and your children relate to "ex-relatives" who are still related through the children?*

5. *What legal, financial, or property matters do you need to consider, in relation to your children and your new marriage? If you have a will, are changes needed in it?*

6. *If you plan to have children, by birth or by adoption, with your new partner, what reactions might your present children have?*

7. *If both partners have children from previous marriages, which residence will you use: his, hers, or a new "neutral" place? What issues are involved in helping the different sets of children blend into one family?*

Your Marriage Is First

A major key to successful parenthood is that you, the spouses, keep the marriage relationship fresh and alive, as the basic bond of the family. When the marriage relationship comes first, you are able to keep the additional demands of parenting in better focus. Regular periods alone together will help you maintain a growing and enjoyable relationship. Finding couple privacy is difficult, yet essential. Many couples schedule at least one night out each week as a couple or with friends. They arrange for good care for their children, and these occasions can be pleasant for both children and parents. Many churches have couples' groups that schedule social activities and provide nurseries and separate activities for the children.

Take the time to encourage your love and romance as a couple. This provides a stronger basis for the love you then can share with your children. As the children mature and leave home, these activities will become even more significant for you.

Parenting Skills

Good parenting does *not* "just happen" or come naturally. Most parents are not formally trained. For better or worse, most learn their skills from childhood family experiences and from talking with relatives and friends and observing the way they relate to their children. In addition, parent education can help improve your parenting skills.

Resources

Several types of parent-education programs may be available in your community. Your church, minister, school, and other community organizations may provide some of these opportunities or give you information about them, and additional resources are listed in the back of this book.

You can use many of the same skills and qualities in parenting that you develop in your husband-wife relationship. For example, patience, forgiveness, empathy, and communication are just as important between parents and children as they are between husband and wife. Expectations, attitudes, and feelings are still the basic elements that guide your behaviors as a parent.

You may need to learn specific information about the normal development of children. Learning which play, reading, and other activities are most helpful at each age also is important. Knowing what to expect from your children at each age and stage gives a healthy perspective to parenting. You will be more comfortable with some difficult times, such as early morning feedings, diaper changing, and having a child say no to you, if you understand that they are part of normal growth. Conflicts, problems, and crises will arise, and knowing how to solve them and where to get assistance when needed makes parenting a more enjoyable adventure. Your family experiences can become times of growth for all concerned, rather than episodes of despair and destructiveness.

Some Parenting Guidelines

Here are three brief principles that will be helpful.

Now Is Most Important

The most important time of your child's life is right now, because it is the only time available for you to be with your children. In order to influence the future, now is the time to share your knowledge and love. The values you give your children will continue through them to others, forming a rich return on the care and love you have invested.

Modeling Is Teaching

Describe the type person you want your child to be, and then be like that person. In this way, your example demonstrates behavior that your child can copy. "What you are speaks so loudly that your children cannot hear what you say." Your children learn most from seeing the way you live every day.

Being a model does not mean you must be perfect. It means that you share yourself with your children. You share the good, and you also show the way you respond when things go wrong and you are less than you would like to be.

Every child needs a sense of love and security, experiences of success, and a good self-image. Dependable care helps your children to feel confident and to succeed in most of their attempts; and successes, whether large or small, enable a child to form a good self-image as a member of a family. Through your example, you teach your children to be competent and capable, so that they can grow comfortably into adulthood.

Children Are Persons

Children have needs and rights similar to yours, modified only by their knowledge and understanding. Like you, they need a balance of structure and freedom. They have a right to privacy and to physical safety. As you involve your children in decisions that affect them and their family, you help them assume responsibility as worthwhile individuals.

Relatives and In-Laws

Triangles can occur between you, your partner, and your children. And, as adult children of your parents, you, your partner, and either set of in-laws may have three-sided conflicts. As you discovered in chapters 2 and 3, you each bring your family members and your experiences into your new relationship of marriage. Parents, brothers, sisters, and other relatives, although they may be absent or deceased, still influence you through the attitudes and habits that you learned with them. These continuing inner voices sometimes are called your "parent tapes." Therefore, it is important that you and your partner continue to talk openly with each other about all your family relationships.

Frequent contact between you, your partner, and relatives provides greater opportunity to be caught between their requests and your own desires. Living near relatives, working at the same place, or having them live in your home brings about complications that you and your partner must resolve together.

You and your partner also probably have some unfinished deep emotional involvements with your parents or other relatives. The arrival of your own children or the aging of your parents may sensitize you especially to these underlying feelings. Most adults move through three stages of relationship to their parents—from dependence in childhood, to independence as adolescents, and finally to interdependence and cooperation, as between equals, in adulthood. Often a person is in some part of each of these three stages, depending upon the issue at hand. Sometimes conflicts between partners result because one partner continues to have excessive emotional dependency on his or her own parents or other relatives.

You need to be free from your parents in the sense of being dependent as their children, so that you can be closer to them as the adults that you are now.

Shifting your relationship from parent/child to adult/adult may be difficult, especially if your parents have their own unresolved emotional investments in you as their children. Assuming adult roles with parents can be more complicated if they have health or housing needs that their adult children are expected to resolve.

Explore: Relations with Relatives

With your partner, discuss issues that are important for you in your interaction with your relatives. Some of these questions may help you in exploring those areas:
1. *Where would you most like to live, in relation to the residences of your parents or other relatives?*
2. *Where and how will, or do, you celebrate holidays, birthdays, and other special occasions? Which would you like to change in some way?*
3. *How do you feel about your relatives? Your blood relations are your partner's in-laws. What difference, if any, does this make in the way you each relate to your partner's relatives? In chapter 2 you may have explored the good and less good characteristics of several important relatives. Talk more about these family members and the way you feel about them.*
4. *What special problems will, or do, you have with certain relatives? Some of these might be: earning more or less than they do; being in a different career or type of work; involvement in a family business or other joint activity; chronic health conditions; family financial obligations; emergencies; differences in life-view and philosophy.*
5. *Are you good friends with your relatives and in-laws? In what ways?*

6. *How have marriages, divorces, deaths, and other changes affected the way you feel about family members? If you have a blended family, with several sets of grandparents and other relatives, how would you like to relate to each set of relatives? Which among these relatives do your children prefer?*
7. *How do you each react to what your parents and other relatives say about your partner or you? In relation to your relatives, what does it mean for you to "forsake all others" for your spouse?*

Extended Family Possibilities

A man leaves his father and his mother and cleaves to his wife, and they become one flesh.   *Genesis 2:24 RSV*

What therefore God has joined together, let not man put asunder.   *Mark 10:9 RSV*

These biblical statements affirm that the covenant of marriage is the central relationship that defines extended families and the relationships between family generations. On the basis of blood and legal ties, an extended family includes single adults, married couples, and children. If you and your partner clearly define these relationships, you can come to appreciate your extended families for the many important positive supports that those persons can share with one another.

In some ways, the church community is similar to the larger extended family. Ideally, the church's emphasis upon love, forgiveness, and concern for all, helps to create a supportive network of caring persons who are available to children and to their parents. Of course, you may have had some negative experiences with some churches that failed to reach these ideals. However, the church community can help you develop many supportive friendships. As part of a church community, you and your partner also can reach out to help others in their times of need.

When relatives are few or live far away, couples who want family support and experiences can obtain these through a church group, or they can organize a family cluster. A family cluster usually includes several couples and their children, as well as single and divorced persons of various ages. Children whose own grandparents are not easily available can benefit from having substitute grandparents in the family cluster, or from other intergenerational activities in a church. This offers ways for couples and their children to participate in a mutual support system of friends, neighbors, and church members. Letters and long distance calls to parents or other relatives also can give support during difficult times and shared happiness in times of joy.

The Possibilities

This poem suggests the dilemmas and opportunities afforded by family members. You and your partner may read it together and talk about your feelings as you review your family relationships, both past and future.

"Wild geese! Wild geese! Mother, do you hear them?"
The barnyard gosling asked from his warm bed.
"Be still, my child, and rest; the dawn is dark;
The air is bleak; the sky is not yet red."
"Mother, why do these lean ones go so fast?"
"Be quiet, my child, for soon we'll get our feed.
We have a shelter and security,
A master who provides for every need."
"Mother, is it great fun to fly so high
And go to any place you'd like to be?"
"Wild geese are fools to risk the hunter's gun
And forage for their food just to be free."
The gosling nestled close to mother's thigh
But dreamed of feathered freedom in the sky.
—*Emory C. Pharr*

Searching

Children and other relatives offer many potential problems, but they also offer unlimited possibilities for growth in love and concern. Your marriage is a part of your individual family systems. Although these often appear to be triangles, with two against one, they provide an opportunity for you and your partner to blend and expand your lives into circles of love and care, with your children and with others. In this way you create your own joint family system. The continuing search for answers to the dilemmas of security versus freedom, concern for self versus concern for others, and the keeping of traditions versus the creation of new traditions, is a part of family relationships.

Marriage is two people agreeing to conduct life
  in ways they both like . . .

Narcisco & Burkett

Like ripples in a pond of water, your marriage reaches out to influence the lives of many others, just as their lives affect you in many ways. With all its privacy and intimacy, marriage is also a social affair, because it is part of the larger social systems around you. Some of these involvements, such as paying taxes, are required, but you choose whether to be a part of many other activities in your community and in the world. Among these are your friendships, community and recreational interests, celebrations, church life, and faith expressions.

Friends

Friendships provide additional opportunities for you to grow individually and as a couple. Friends who are common to both partners provide needed emotional support and companionship. Many couples often are closer to their friends, both married and single, than to most relatives. Common interests and the easy access provided by being neighbors are typical bases for forming friendships. When you have mutual friends, there is more opportunity for couple activities. Enduring values are gained by married persons as they associate with other couples and maintain several mutual friendships.

Not all your friends will be mutual. Since you and your partner are individuals and have your own interests, it is enriching for each of you to have some separate friendships. These may develop around hobbies, recreational activities, social clubs, or job-related interests. Sharing your experiences from these friendships can expand the quality of your marriage.

Sometimes a lack of friendships may suggest that you are uncomfortable with oher persons. If you do not have other friends, too heavy a burden may be placed upon your partner to provide all the emotional support you need.

Explore: Friends

With your partner, take some time to consider the way your friendships relate to your marriage. Use these questions to guide you:

1. *Select two or three friends who have meant much to you. Describe the qualities you value in each friend. You might tell your partner about the most enjoyable or the funniest experience you had with each friend.*
2. *Which of your friends does your partner especially like or dislike? Do you dislike any of your partner's friends? Describe the feelings you each have about these friends.*
3. *Are there times when you prefer to be with your friend(s) rather than with your partner? In what ways do these times help or threaten your relationship?*
4. *Do you or your partner discuss "private" matters with any friends? Is this acceptable to you? . . . to your partner?*
5. *Do you and your partner quarrel or disagree in the presence of friends? When? Does either of you try to out-talk, control, embarrass the other, or do you act differently when your friends are present? How do each of you feel about these times?*
6. *Which activities do you enjoy doing with friends—individually and as a couple?*
7. *What are your agreements, or ground rules, concerning possible sexual facets of friendships? Does either of you worry about a possible sexual or romantic involvement of your partner with others? How might loneliness, feelings of rejection, or other emotional factors affect your friendships? Talk about your feelings and reactions in these areas.*
8. *What expressions of warmth, appreciation, and*

affection are appropriate between you and your friends? . . . between your partner and his or her friends?

9. *Does time you each spend with friends interfere with your relationship as partners? If so, describe when this happens and how you would like to change it.*

10. *Do your friendships include persons from several racial and ethnic groups? How do your friendships express your values and goals? In what way are your friendships related to your community, church, or career involvements?*

Community, Leisure, and Recreation

You may choose to use your free time in community, recreational, and other leisure activities. You may use it to relax, to help others, and as an opportunity for personal growth and education.

Community involvement refers to activities designed to make your community a better place to live. Some may be causes that are important to you, such as environmental concerns, alternate energy sources, or health improvement. You may help your community by leading an organized group of children or youth, as part of a church or community agency. You may take part in political, labor, management, or civic committees.

Recreation includes individual and group sports, hobbies, crafts, and other interests that offer an enjoyable change of pace. These are ways you "re-create" yourself. Some, such as tennis, require two people, while others, such as fishing or bicycle riding, can be done alone. Some types of recreation require travel and may be expensive, while others can be done at home or may cost nothing.

Leisure refers to all your free time—the time when you are not working at your job. In addition to the time you invest in your community and in recreation, each partner needs some personal time. Leisure can be a time to relax, rest, or do nothing, or it can be used for couple, family, and friendship activities. Leisure can be an opportunity for meditation and self-renewal.

Explore: Leisure Activities

Allow time to discuss the way you each use your leisure time. Here are some possible areas to consider:

1. *In which community service activities do you participate? What would you like to do for your community?*

2. *To which charitable, service, and community causes do you give money? Do you agree on the amounts to contribute?*

3. *How much money do you spend on recreation, sports, and hobbies? Do you agree on these expenses?*

4. *Which of your recreational activities help to maintain or improve your health? In what ways? Does your health or physical condition limit your recreational activities? How have you adjusted to these limitations?*

5. *What does each partner enjoy for recreation? First, let one partner describe the activities you think the other enjoys; then let the other partner comment on the description.*

6. *Which activities do you enjoy together? Which ones do you prefer to do alone?*

7. *Do you have hobbies, crafts, or arts that are fulfilling and enjoyable for you? Talk about these. How do you each want your partner to relate to these?*

8. *Does either of you ever feel left out of the exciting activities in which your partner participates? When? In what ways? Share your feelings about these times.*

9. *How frequently and how well do you carry out the "fine art of doing nothing"? Can you relax without worrying about anything? How do you do this?*

10. *When do you enjoy being alone? How much time should be "personal time" for each of you to do things separately, as individuals? What are your arrangements for personal time? When do you enjoy being with others?*

11. *When is leisure time an empty time or a burden for you? How do you fill up empty time? Are you uncomfortable when you are alone?*

12. *Describe the way you would like to change your use of leisure time. Share your feelings about these activities.*

Holidays, Celebrations, Symbols

Holidays and celebrations can be times for renewal, refreshment, and the achievement of new visions of the milestones in your history. They also offer opportunities to reaffirm your relationship with friends, relatives, your community, and the world. These special days can provide the common experiences that help to unify couples, families, and communities.

* HOLIDAYS *

Holidays, from "holy days," are important reminders of events in our common history, and they can be important for couple or family activities, as well. For partners whose relatives are near, there can be a reunion and the sharing of experiences. Holidays spent with friends can be enjoyable, too.

Holidays may be times of increased tension for some couples. Since there is often more time to be together, the opportunity for conflict increases, also. Some persons may feel sad or depressed because of unresolved inner feelings, or because others seem to be so much happier or more successful. Children are usually out of school on holidays, and this may create more stress for some parents.

* CELEBRATIONS *

To celebrate means to honor, to proclaim, to extol, and to sound the praises of someone or of some event. On their birthdays, you can honor and praise the life of each person in the family and of each of your friends. Through these celebrations, relatives and friends can tell a person how important he or she is to them.

Your wedding anniversary is another special day. It can be an occasion to renew your commitment and to share your appreciation for being with each other.

Worship in your home is also a celebration. In worship, you give "worth-ship" to God in appreciation for the gifts of life and love. You may celebrate God's continuous love to you and to others with a prayer at mealtime, by reading from the Bible and from devotional materials, by sharing poems and inspiring thoughts for the day, and through music and other art forms. It is helpful to have a worship celebration each day, as an opportunity to grow in love and appreciation of each other, of other persons, and of God.

* SYMBOLS *

Symbols remind us of important persons and groups in our lives. They point to realities beyond themselves.

Symbols help us express who we are and what we value. They help us form common bonds with others who share the same values.

You and your partner have some symbols that are special for you. Pictures, clothing, rings, gifts, and music help recall special events in your lives and bring you closer together.

Explore: Symbols and Meanings

Together, talk about holidays, celebrations, and symbols that have special meanings for you. Here are some possible areas:

1. *What is your favorite holiday? In what way is it important to your marriage?*
2. *Do your holidays involve your relatives or friends? When do job responsibilities prevent you from enjoying some holidays?*
3. *What did each of your childhood families celebrate? Share some special memories of family celebrations. How do these influence the celebrations you and your partner have?*
4. *Together, look at pictures or other symbols of your relationship. How do these remind you of past experiences or future goals?*
5. *Do you have special music that you think of as "our song"? Talk about the words and what the music means for you.*
6. *What other symbols are important for you?*

Art forms may remind you of important events and values in your lives. Music, photographs, paintings, and sculpture help you celebrate your human relationships. Again and again, symbols call you to renew your awareness of the many ways in which God and other persons care for you. Symbols also may remind you to reach out to others with care, concern, love, and encouragement.

Church Possibilities

The church is God's witness in today's world, supporting the best in life and calling attention to the needs of persons and groups. In this age of technology, leisure, professionalism, and self-interest, God continues to call the church to its servant existence. As individuals, as couples, and as families, you continually are called to be a part of God's exciting work today; you are invited to invest your lives.

Jesus pointed to the excitement and joy of a wedding to describe the importance of continuing our relationship with God and with one another in the Christian community of faith. Some instances of his teachings are in Matthew 9:15, 22:8-12, 25:1-13; Mark 2:19; and John 2:1-11. When we embrace the Christian faith, we indicate that we wish to participate in the Christian community as the Body of Christ.

Religion and church involvement have unique meanings for each of you. Since a local church is both a religious and a social organization, it provides important ways for you to develop friendships, become involved in your community, and worship God.

Your religious background and church activity probably fit into one of these categories:

a. partners from same denomination or tradition
b. partners from different Protestant denominations
c. one partner Protestant, the other Roman Catholic, Jewish, or other religious tradition
d. one partner from a church tradition, the other not involved in any religious group
e. neither partner involved in any religious group

You can benefit by considering the ways your previous religious experiences affect your decisions about your church involvement as a couple.

We think it is important that you both be involved in a local church in your community. That involvement will call you out of your selfish isolation, and your genuine love as a couple will lead you to share your lives with others. As a by-product, participation in the church can enrich your own relationship, as well.

Expressing Your Personal Faith

Your personal faith includes your life philosophy, your perspectives toward life, and your own assumptions about yourself and others, which you express in your daily conversation and actions. You may have a formal creed or other statement of faith, but your attitudes, values, and expectations eventually are expressions of your personal faith.

Your faith is your relationship with others—the world. Your faith can be "bad" or "sour" if you assume that the universe is unfriendly and threatening. It becomes trust and confidence when you experience the world and other persons as being friendly and supportive to you as an individual. Whatever your beliefs, they are based upon your life experiences thus far. Out of those experiences you decide to trust, or not to trust, others and God. Your faith involves your hopes and decisions. By using the communication skills presented earlier, you can clarify your personal faith in discussions with your partner.

Explore: Ways You Express Faith

Allow time when you can talk together about your personal faith. Some of these questions may help you to share these areas with each other:

1. What basic beliefs do you each have? How do you apply them?

2. On which facets of your personal faiths do you and your partner agree? Where do you disagree? How do you use these beliefs to grow in your understanding of each other and of life?

3. In what ways do you participate in the Christian community now? As a couple, what kind of church involvement would you like? Will (or do) you participate in the same local church? When both partners are not active in the same church, they miss opportunities to be together and to develop friendships with other couples who share similar beliefs and values.

Here are some types of group involvement that could be expressions of your personal faith. Describe how you would like to be involved in some of these.

1. Sunday worship and church school classes or groups
2. study and fellowship groups in church
3. church committees and work groups
4. health, welfare, and civic improvement groups
5. political parties and political-action groups
6. the arts and charitable, scientific, and environmental causes
7. social clubs, fraternal orders, service clubs, secret orders
8. groups to help children, youth, senior citizens, handicapped, etc.

Talk about which of these you would like to take part in as a couple and which each partner would like to do individually. In what ways do these involvements express your personal faiths?

Special Growth Experiences

Some personal experiences are so compelling and impressive that a person will rearrange life perspectives around them. These peak experiences are like being on a mountain from which, in symbolic terms, an individual is given a more direct contact with God and is provided a broader viewpoint from which to interpret life and marriage.

It may be difficult to describe your special peak experiences. Symbols and stories may help label intense feelings, but it may be impossible to describe them completely. For some persons, religious terms can be used to describe these very personal encounters; other persons may use scientific, artistic, or mystical terminology.

You and your partner will grow and achieve deeper levels of intimacy when you share some of your special, most meaningful experiences. The next EXPLORE suggests a way to do this.

Explore: Personal Faith Experiences

In this exercise, it is very important that each of you listens with respect as the other describes his or her experience. Encourage each other in sharing, yet be careful not to push your partner to share more than she or he wishes to express. Some of these questions may help you to explore your peak experiences:

1. *What peak experiences have you had? When? How often? Where?*
2. *What made this experience so special for you?*
3. *In what ways has this helped you to understand and appreciate yourself, your partner, others, the universe, and/or God?*
4. *What sense of mystery, amazement, or ecstasy accompanied your experience? Do these feelings continue now?*
5. *What changes have there been in your life because of this experience?*

Everyone Is Everywhere!

The rhythms and polarities of marriage transport you and your partner from intimate sexual and personal intercourse, to social intercourse with the whole world. Living "happily ever after" cannot be done in isolation from others. Your marriage expresses your personalities. It is related to your jobs and your careers, to your relatives and friends, and to your world, the universe, and God. Through the lens of your marriage, you can see other persons with new vision and choose the ways you will relate to them. In marriage, partners can "be everything to each other" only for brief periods. You need others, and they need you. The whole world is at your door.

Chapter 10
Sneak Preview
of Years Ahead

Where do we grow from here?
. . . expectations are never quite the same as reality.

Please tell me you love me again;
. . . it's always so nice to know.

Exchanging vows at your wedding ceremony is simple, compared with the work and the joy of bringing those vows to reality in your daily lives together. The focus of this chapter will assume that you have been married for at least a few months. If you are only anticipating your wedding, you may wish to review this chapter later.

Your marriage has brought many minor and major changes in your lives. As noted in chapter 5, change, either planned or unplanned, creates stress. Not all the issues you explored were settled before your wedding, but you now have the opportunity to work toward mutually satisfactory solutions to those, and to the new issues that will arise.

It is reassuring to remember that even successful couples have differences of opinions and occasional conflicts. Your sincere commitment to stay together and to work on troublesome issues is only the beginning chapter in your relationship. The joy of being together in warm and reassuring moments makes your efforts worthwhile. This combination of commitment and satisfaction probably is the difference between couples who succeed in marriage and those who give up. Building on the positives in your marriage lays the foundation for facing the negatives honestly and with hope.

There are many issues that newly married couples face in the first few months. It is helpful to take a long-range view of your years ahead in order to put daily events into a better perspective. A specific event may make your marriage appear to be going down . . . . However, when you and your

partner take a larger view, you may find that many good things are happening, and your overall perspective may look more like this:

up . . up . . . up . . down . . up . . . up . . . up . . down . . . up

As a married couple, you can give yourselves permission to disagree and to have your ups and downs, but each partner also can be open to accept the apology, forgiveness, and warmth of the other. Marriage, in large measure, probably is a self-fulfilling prophecy. This means that in your marriage, you more or less produce what you expect to happen. Your resources, attitudes, and skills for communicating love and solving problems are essential tools to be used to create the quality of marriage you would like.

Explore: Ups and Downs

Take some quiet time together to look at your total relationship since you met, or during the past several months. Let each partner independently draw a line, as on a graph, to show the way you view your relationship. Show the ups and downs and the general direction of your relationship during that time. Note the "down" periods and the especially good times. When you have completed your lines, compare them and talk about some of the details.

In many ways, you and your partner are really on your own. At times this may seem frightening, yet you can reach out to comfort and support each other as you develop. You may agree that you will never go to sleep while you are angry. You may not solve the problem that night, but you can agree to talk about it later.

68

Some Pre- and Postwedding Concerns

After reading through the following issues that couples may face during the first weeks or months of their marriage, use the EXPLORE exercise to examine your feelings about those that you face. If you are not married, try to imagine how you would react. If you are now married, consider how you are handling these issues.

Your Name

The traditional assumption in our culture has been that the wife assumes her husband's name. For many couples, this is no longer the case. Some choose to call themselves by the husband's last name, some by a combination of both last names, some by the wife's name, and some choose a name different from either family name. The new name may be from another time, another language, or it may signify some experience the couple has had. Whatever your choice, your name can be an expression of your mutual identity. Your name carries great emotional investment.

For some women, a professional name is helpful or even necessary. A wife may choose to use her maiden name in her career, in addition to the name she and her husband choose for themselves as a couple. This can provide the woman with a clear career identity, separate from her marriage.

Your Residence

For most couples, marriage means that one or both partners must move to a new residence. Selecting a place to live can be difficult, as you consider the advantages and disadvantages of various locations. Moving involves planning and work. The many details to be considered can produce fatigue and stress that may affect your relationship.

If both partners move to a new residence, then each of you can feel that the residence really is "ours" from the beginning. The many decisions needed to make it "feel like home" probably will be made jointly. If you live in a residence that belonged to one partner before your wedding, it might be more difficult for the other partner to become fully involved in some of the household decisions.

Memories

How will you preserve the pictures and other reminders of your wedding? Your wedding is one of the milestones of the life that you share together. Remembering your wedding also may encourage you to renew your hopes and aspirations together.

In addition to saving photographs and tape recordings, many couples freeze some of their wedding cake or other refreshments. On their first anniversary, they remember their wedding as they enjoy the cake. However, it requires planning to save remembrances.

Roles and Responsibilities

You are free to organize your home any way you wish. Many persons have difficulty believing that they really are free to create their own life-style in ways that are unique for them. The effort to make your marriage fit the marriage pattern of your parents, relatives, or friends can cause many problems. The statement, "My family never did it that way," is sure to complicate your marriage. Working together, you and your partner can establish your own responsibilities and modify your roles as seems best for both of you.

There are no tasks, duties, or roles that are automatically "supposed to be" done by the wife or by the husband. As spouses, you each agree to assume responsibilities according to your skills and interests. Few persons like to wash dishes, clean bathrooms, or carry out garbage, yet these and other menial jobs are part of housekeeping, whether you are married or single. Together, you can consider all the details of homemaking and agree to share the unpleasant as well as the pleasant responsibilities.

As you gain experience, you probably will need to revise the roles that you established initially. You can talk over your feelings about the way you have organized your responsibilities. When conflicts occur, you can use your communication and problem-solving skills to improve your procedures.

Energy and Activity Levels

You may have noticed that on some days, you are more alert and active than on others. Each of you has several cycles of physical and psychological functioning that are influenced by body makeup and by events around you. Personal rhythms are unique for each of you, but they are not as fixed as some would have you believe. Shifts in your mood and energy levels can underlie some of the ups and downs in your relationship.

Here are some patterns that affect the way you and your partner relate to each other. When these cycles fit together, you will respond in a different manner than in those periods when you are at opposite ends of your cycles.

1. *Wakefulness and sleep.* Each of you typically is more awake and alert during some parts of the day. Persons require different amounts of sleep in order to feel well rested. If one partner needs more sleep, the other can consider this in arranging his or her waking time. A partner may be an early riser, a "day person," or a "night owl." You may need to coordinate your sexual activities with your energy and sleep cycles.
2. *Stimulation and quietness.* You and your partner may prefer different types of stimulation at various times. One may enjoy a loud radio, much television, and more noise, excitement, and activity than the other likes. At some times, each of you may want more physical contact, hugging, and caressing than usual. One of you may prefer more quiet and solitude, and activities such as reading or crafts. As you each seek the type of stimulation you prefer, consider your partner's desires.
3. *Energy levels.* Some couples have more energy than others, and in each marriage, one partner may have more or less energy at certain times than the other. If your partner says "I'm too tired" or "Let's liven up the place," you may feel resentful or unappreciated. Energy levels also are related to jobs, sleep, food intake, and general health.
4. *Activity patterns.* Some persons always prefer to be "on the go," while others would rather relax at home with hobbies or other quiet activities. If you and your partner have similar activity patterns, fewer disagreements will arise. You each may be engaged separately at some times during the week and plan to do things together at other times. In some marriages, partners agree to go their own ways, and this is quite satisfactory for them. Other couples plan a big night out each weekend. Although all couples develop their own patterns, the important common element is that the partners agree on the pattern.

Physical Limitations

In addition to the above factors, some couples may need to adjust to the physical limitations of one or both partners. Chronic conditions, such as a dysfunctioning body organ or restrictions on the ability to walk, talk, or participate in activities may be a part of some marriages. Even if you and your partner have no major physical limitations, you may need to

consider these factors when you engage in joint activities with your friends.

High Hopes Before Your Wedding Versus What You Are Now Experiencing

Some behaviors or habits of your mate may surprise, annoy, or disappoint you. By contrast, you may believe that none of *your* habits has a negative effect on your partner! Sometimes the unrealistic hope that marriage will solve all personal problems leads to criticism or dissatisfaction. It is important to keep your dreams up to date and talk with your partner about your feelings. We hope that you have explored many areas of your relationship already, so that there will be few unpleasant surprises. However, there still may be some things that annoy you. These may range all the way from "squeezing the toothpaste tube" to money, sex, jobs, or relatives and friends. You can take one of two basic approaches to these concerns, depending upon how you each view your marriage.

A Losing Plan

You can choose to add all the little and big differences together and interpret them as making you unhappy. In any marriage, either partner can probably find reason enough to create grounds for divorce, if that person has decided to end the marriage. It takes both partners to make the marriage successful, but it takes only one to make the marriage fail.

A Winning Plan

The preferable approach to disillusionment in marriage is based on your covenant with each other that you will accept disappointments as a part of your marriage and that you will seek to improve your relationship. You may consider each difference and assign it to one of these three categories:

a. differences that are not worth mentioning, so you show your love to your partner by overlooking these minor habits or behaviors
b. differences you cannot solve at the moment because of circumstances or risk, so you hope to talk about them at some future time
c. differences you and your partner can discuss comfortably and resolve immediately

At times, one partner may seem to develop faster in some ways. Even if you dislike certain of your partner's habits, you can focus on the good qualities and build on those. As you create many good experiences together, some differences may not seem important enough to risk damaging your relationship by trying to solve them now. This covenantal approach signifies that you choose to stay together. You decide to love each other as you are, rather than requiring that either partner change in order to have the other's love. From this perspective, disappointments can become opportunities for growth.

To resolve differences, you may change your expectations, your behaviors, or both. Disagreements are a step toward establishing your personal limits versus couple limits. Respect for genuine personal differences is an important factor in your lives together. Diverse perspectives keep partners alive, awake, and sensitive to each other, and dealing with them offers each of you the opportunity to affirm, forgive, and broaden your love. This deepening love can hold you together through rough, as well as in happy times. When you live this covenant, you are saying to your partner, "I care deeply about you, and I will continue to be here with you."

Dreams and Hopes

To keep your marriage fresh and alive, it is essential to emphasize and build upon the positive elements in your relationship. You will need leisurely times together, during which you can dream aloud about your future and share your hopes and wishes. An exciting mystery of marriage is the continual awakening in each partner of the potential for love, growth, and new accomplishments. Sharing your hopes and dreams can bring you closer together and encourage greater teamwork in your marriage.

Explore: Life-style and Hope

Plan some talk time, and together, review the various issues mentioned in this chapter. Decide which of these, or other issues, you will explore. Here are some guides:

1. *Consider the sound of "Mr. and Mrs. _____" in contrast to "Mrs. and Mr. _____." Does the order of your names make any difference to you? How does your name or the combination of names express the way you see your marriage and yourselves?*
2. *How long will you be in your current residence? How do you feel about moving? What moving or household-*

arrangement differences have you had? How do you resolve these?
3. *How do you preserve and use wedding memories and other memories?*
4. *How have you assigned homemaking responsibilities? What changes would you like to make now? How do you feel about these?*
5. *Which partner enjoys more stimulation? Who would rather talk? . . . listen? How do you cope with loss of energy, fatigue, or sickness? What happens when one partner's cycles seem to interfere with the other's rhythms or desires?*
6. *What physical or skill limitations affect your marriage? How do you feel about these?*
7. *When you feel you would like to leave your marriage, what do you do about it? In what way can you talk about this with your partner or with others?*
8. *Describe the greatest fear, worry, or concern you have about your marriage. Share how you feel about each other and try to eliminate the source of your fear.*
9. *Describe two or three hopes and dreams you have for your marriage. Talk about ways you can accomplish these in the next months or years.*

Some Ways to Grow

Increasingly, various types of marriage enrichment and other marriage-education opportunities are available to couples at every stage of their married life. Through these, you can receive encouragement, improve your skills as a couple, and share your insights with other couples. You also can benefit from using couple-relationship inventories, such as the *Mirror*, which help you examine your marriage as you each see it and as each of you thinks your partner sees it.

We urge you to participate in couple growth opportunities as a recurring part of your marriage. Talk with your pastor about using these resources and consult the references in the back of this book.

A Very Long-Range View

During your married life, you and your partner will experience several definite periods. After many years, it may even seem that you have had three or four "marriages" to the same person, because you both have changed. Sometimes you may wish that your spouse were like she or he "used to be." Of course, this is not possible, because of the changes within yourselves, the changes in your relatives and friends, in your career and work, and even in the world around you. There will be changes in the way each of you looks at your marriage, but these are to be expected and encouraged. Because of those changes, you will know that you are growing.

Expecting the Unexpected

Together, the days that you shape add up to the years of marriage you will share. Across those years, you can expect some changes to produce unexpected crises. A crisis is not the event itself, but your interpretation of the event. Usually when a crisis occurs, you have reached a point where you cannot cope well with this one additional situation. What happens is important, but your reactions to the happening are even more critical in relation to the outcome.

In most of life's events, partners have a sense of being in control. In a crisis, you may feel that you have lost control of your life and your marriage, but you have the power to turn a crisis into a time for growth. This is done by using your skills and working with your partner and others who can help you. Sometimes you may need to pull back from events for a while, so that you can regroup your resources and cope more effectively with life.

Looking Ahead

Crises and changes become less threatening when you take a long-range view of your marriage. Many family and adult development specialists describe our adult years as a series of stages, with special experiences that tend to take place at each stage.

Ages and Stages in Marriage

Stages in marriage typically are related to the personal experiences of each partner, the partners' stage of career development as noted in chapter 7, and the ages of their children, if any. Your calendar age is less important than the types of events that are occurring in your lives. For example, there is nothing magic about age 30 or age 40. However, if you believe that life is over for you when you leave age 29, or age 39, then you may perceive that birthday as a crisis.

The much more important issue is whether you are where you want to be and who you want to be, at each stage of your life and of your marriage. Again, your judgment of your success depends upon whether your real life matches your expectations.

Family Stages

For couples who have children, family stages may be described in relation to the ages of the children—especially the oldest and the youngest. Couples who are experiencing pregnancy or the excitement of preschool children will enjoy associating with others who are in the same general stage. They can swap stories, share child care, and exchange toys and clothes. In this way they provide mutual support in learning about and coping with parenting. Turning points in marriage also occur when the first child enters elementary school, when children reach adolescence. When the last child enters school, and when the last child graduates. Many details of these stages are available in books such as Duvall.

Stages in your marriage also may be marked by major job and career changes, a move from one community to another, the death of a close relative or special friend, or by significant changes in your health. Your career-stage cycles interact with your marriage stages, but none of these is a final determination of your happiness. You and your partner can use these changes to strengthen your relationship.

Planning Ahead

One way to discuss the stages in your marriage is to add together several events so as to make a meaningful interpretation of a longer period in your lives. Your expectations and goals guide you toward some events, and away from others. It is helpful to be clear about the events each of you considers to be most significant. It is very important to be clear about your expectations, because, as noted in chapter 3, you probably will act on the basis of those expectations. Your picture of your future is very important for your marriage today.

Explore: Your Timelines

For this exercise you will need some paper and at least an hour to talk. First, together, draw a very long line to represent the time from now until your retirement, or beyond—the rest of your life. Along your line, mark some important events that each of you hopes will have happened by the time you reach a certain age. Some of these may be joint events and others may affect only one partner. Then

add other probable events that may influence your marriage. Some of these might be the things your parents or other relatives may be doing by the time you reach a particular age. Some markers may be alternate, or second-choice, goals. Your timeline might look something like the one on the facing page.

Ages:	20s	30s	40s	50s	60s & beyond
	Complete educations	Move to "permanent" residence	Another move to improve career status	Last child graduates from school	It really is worth the effort!
	Big trip before children come	All the children are now in school!	Wondering whether it is all worth it	Period of maximum income	Retirement/Re-engagement
	Coming of children	Becoming more active in community affairs	Possible changes in career/work	Becoming grandparents/grandpeople!	
		Career advancements	Doing more things "as a couple"		

These examples of phrases to identify periods in your lives are more general than yours will be. As you talk about your future, try to be specific about what you want or do not want to happen at each age. Discuss your feelings about looking at your whole lives together. Share dreams, hopes, and desires. At times, hug and touch each other as you talk.

On Having a Dual-Control Marriage

A dual-control electric blanket may suggest two key sets of factors in your marriage:

a. warmth, affection, and love
b. control, power, skills, and abilities

A dual-control marriage, like a dual-control blanket, provides the desired warmth for each partner, and each partner is able to adjust situations for maximum comfort as she or he perceives it. You each express affection and control in every encounter, conversation, and event of your marriage.

By identifying that which you consider to be good and desirable, you then can decide how you will reach those desired goals. You and your partner really can be in control of your future together. This is tremendously freeing and exciting because it means that you can choose to stay together, just as you might choose to separate. Together, in your dual-control marriage, you can blend your lives as you please.

Finding the Real You

At each stage in your marriage, you will discover that in every communication and event, there is always one more layer of meaning and intention underneath the layer you express. Eventually, you may reach through most of the layers to the real you. This is the reason for our emphasis upon your covenant in marriage. We hope that each of you continues to affirm the other. You may wish to read the following statement aloud.

I want the best for you, for me, and for us. If it does not seem that way in this event, then I'll try again. Down deep, I really do love and care for you, for me, for us, and for others. I accept you as you really are now. This is what I mean when I say that I love you.

Chapter 11
What Good Is a Wedding?

If there is righteousness in the heart,
    there will be beauty in the character.
If there is beauty in the character,
    there will be harmony in the home.
If there is harmony in the home,
    there will be order in the nation.
When there is order in each nation,
    there will be peace in the world.*
We believe the source of it all is God.

An Old Chinese Proverb

Your wedding does not have a money-back guarantee. Neither does it have a provision for exchanging your spouse, in case he or she does not measure up to all your anticipations. No longer can a person purchase a spouse, nor does either partner own the other, as property or as a servant.

The previous chapters have invited you, as partners, to explore many facets of marriage. If you are anticipating your wedding, this chapter can help you to examine some meanings of Christian marriage and to express them in your wedding. If you are already married, it can be used to review and refresh your understandings of your wedding, in relation to your marriage. In this way, you can renew your wedding vows, either in private or with others.

Since the concept of covenant is so important in Christian marriage, you may want to review its definition in chapter 1.

Some Christian Understandings of Marriage

Christians have many different understandings of marriage; therefore, there is no one correct Christian way to view it. In the light of these perspectives, you and your partner can use the following statements to develop your own meanings of your wedding and of your marriage.

The church holds marriage to be a sacred covenant relationship—not a mere dull legalistic institution. Marriage is a dynamic, growing interaction, between spouses who faithfully love and cherish each other.

Marriage as a covenant between spouses is modeled upon God's covenant of unconditional love with Israel, and with all people, through Jesus Christ. This promise of love and grace is supremely expressed in the appearance of Jesus as the Christ, the Messiah—God present in the world.

To Wed Is to Covenant

The root word "wed" means "to covenant, promise, pledge, or vow." The now-seldom-used "troth" suggests faith, fidelity, and truth. Marriage is one way to express ourselves as persons before God. It is a relationship through which we can learn more about love. Because of this, marriage is a parable of God's relationship to the world. The continuing concern of spouses for each other can become an example of this trust (Mal. 2:10-16). The wedding feast was used by Jesus to suggest the excitement and joy between ourselves and God (Mark 2:19; Matt. 25:1-13; John 2:9, 3:29; Rev. 18:23).

The church believes that marriage is one of several life-styles that a Christian may choose in response to God's love. God cares for us all, just as we are, whether single, married, widowed, or divorced. The focus of this guide is upon marriage, and we assume either that you are considering marriage—whether or not you marry each other—or that you are married already. This does not imply, however, that from a Christian perspective, marriage is to be preferred by everyone. Most Christians accept an intentional decision to live as a single person as being just as valid as a decision to marry.

Adequate understanding and affirmation of oneself, whether single or married, is essential to wholesome living. As a Christian, the good news is that God loves you. God has created you and given you the power, within limits, to control and shape your world and your life as you choose. Creative growth is a lifetime process, and God sustains you in every circumstance, even though you may be unaware of this grace.

Each event calls for caring and loving relationships; many passages in the New Testament describe this "more excellent way of love" (Luke 10:29-37; Rom. 12; I Cor. 13; I John 4). In Paul's discussions of marriage in Ephesians 5:21-33 and in Colossians 3:18-21, he gives examples of unconditional love in marriage and family relationships. Compared to life in ancient times, Paul's model of marriage was a big step forward.

Wife and Husband as Equals

Our deeper understanding of the equality of men and women today emphasizes wife and husband as equal partners, who give unqualified love to each other. Together, they can choose models for their marriage that will allow them to express that love most fully. Each model may differ from the others, but when unconditional love is present, all can be genuine expressions of Christian marriage.

Marriage may be described as the joining of two persons into "one flesh." In one Creation story this statement appears: "Therefore a man leaves his father and mother and cleaves to his wife, and they become one flesh. And the man and his wife were both naked, and were not ashamed" (Gen. 2:24 RSV). Today we may wish that a parallel also had been written—namely, that a woman leaves her parents and cleaves to her husband. The intent, however, is clear. If a woman and a man choose to covenant in marriage, their first loyalty is to each other, and all other loyalties must be ordered by this. "Two becoming one, yet two persons" in marriage, illustrates the richness of God's offering to us.

"One flesh" implies much more than sexual intercourse, although that act is included in the expression. Important as it is, it takes more than sexual interest to maintain a marriage. Common goals, the same residence, affectional and personal needs, and relations with relatives and friends—all are involved in the covenant of marriage. Perhaps the term "body" may better express this broader meaning of one flesh, in that marriage resembles a legal corporate body which functions as one unit, yet has individual members.

Some use "one flesh" to suggest that because persons marry, they must think alike, act alike, always agree, do everything together, and become carbon copies of each other. On the contrary, into the one body of marriage, each partner brings a uniqueness that enriches both partners, and Christian marriage assumes that both have equal rights and responsibilities.

Growing in Marriage

Marriage may be seen as Christian nurture and growth. The inner qualities of each person are expressed in the way that he or she treats others. Usually an individual's behavior at home extends outward into the community, as suggested by the proverb quoted at the beginning of this chapter.

Your adult development is not complete at the time of your wedding, or even after ten or twenty years of marriage. Your marriage is a laboratory, or workshop, in which you can help each other continue to grow, guided by your best understandings of God's wishes. Prayers, devotionals, Bible readings, and hymn-singing are obvious "religious" expressions. They are important as part of Christian nurture in your home, but even more essential are your expressions of love, kindness, consideration, and other "fruits of God's Spirit." In your marriage, you live your faith in God through your intimate daily contacts. This is active religion. Knowing that you really accept each other, you can grow beyond many feelings of guilt that yours is not a "perfect" marriage. Christian marriage assumes that each partner accepts full responsibility for the creation of love and trust among family members.

As spouses, your intention to support and love each other "until death" refers not so much to a length of time as to a way of living. One by-product of unconditional love is the permanence of the partnership—persons tend to remain in relationships that are enjoyable, uplifting, and supportive. This fidelity in marriage is a matter of being faithful to God and, on this basis, of responding to family members with love and concern.

Commitment Gives Freedom

Your sincere commitment to each other gives you freedom to evaluate past ways of doing things, so that you can improve yourselves and your marriage. It gives you freedom to be yourselves, freedom to withdraw occasionally from each other for personal renewal and insight, and freedom to be open and honest without destroying your relationship. Because of your commitment, both of you can continue to develop and grow throughout your lives. Your basic unconditional pledge is the foundation of your willingness to work out whatever difficulties you may encounter. This kind of grace in marriage really is amazing.

Marriage is not an end in itself, but one means toward a goal—the development of the persons involved. Through marriage, a fuller quality of living can be achieved. Because of the love that partners find with each other, they can look beyond themselves and reach out to others in the world.

Marriage is like a sacrament. Christian sacraments are events that express God's acceptance of persons into new relationships in the Christian community. Although most Protestant Christians consider baptism and the Lord's Supper as official sacraments, marriage also can have a sacramental quality. This happens when partners fully accept each other into the two-person community of Christian marriage. Children, other relatives, and friends also benefit from the quality of mutual affirmation that the marriage relationship demonstrates. The wedding can be one expression of your commitment to manifest God's love, grace, and forgiveness in your marriage.

The key concept in these understandings of Christian marriage is God's continuing unquestioning love and the couple's sharing of this love with each other and with others. This covenantal model includes at least two basic elements. The first is the mutual intention of the partners to love and to cherish each other. From this comes the second—their mutual commitment to work, through their relationship in love, for their own growth and for the growth of others.

Expressing Christian Understandings in Your Wedding Service

Whether simple or elaborate, your wedding service should have a particular meaning for you and your partner. It should be more than just a ceremony, because it points to the many facets of marriage. Your wedding assumes that you and your partner have explored those areas thoroughly and have chosen to enter marriage as an expression of your self-understandings and your love for each other, in the context of God's love for you. Here are some possible special meanings that the wedding ceremony may have for a couple:

a. a public statement of the intentional, voluntary pledge made by both partners

b. an acknowledgment of God's grace and presence in support of the marriage covenant

c. a separation from childhood homes and from parents and other relatives, because the marriage covenant is now the primary relationship

d. a reminder of their preparation for marriage, which has involved private conversations together, meetings with a pastor, and all that the partners have learned from families, friends, and other sources.

Explore: Meanings of Marriage

Allow some time to discuss concepts of marriage. One possibility is for each partner to mark one of the preceding paragraphs and then to talk about its meaning for you as a couple. You may read some of the references from the Bible and talk about how they relate to your marriage. In your discussions with your pastor, you may want to talk about some of these concepts.

Independently, each of you can write some words or phrases that express what your marriage and your wedding mean to you; then you can compare notes. You also might locate pictures, cartoons, or other materials that will help you talk about your wedding.

Some persons consider that a wedding signifies a loss of freedom; that it is a mere ceremony so that you may show off to others; or that it means the end of happy times. Some may assume that the wedding ceremony, or the marriage license, entitles one to insult or mistreat one's partner in the privacy of the home. Share any negative views of marriage that might bother you now.

Some Wedding Details

Your wedding service is both a religious ceremony and a legal proceeding. The exact requirements for marriage vary among the states, so you and your partner should consult with your pastor and/or appropriate public official concerning the legalities in your state. Here are some details to check:

1. Where is the marriage license secured? (This usually is in the same county in which the wedding service is to be held.)
2. Does each partner meet the age, residence, and other requirements for marriage in your state?
3. Is a blood test or other physical checkup required in order to obtain a marriage license, and are there time restrictions involved? (This is also a good time to have a more complete physical examination, if you have not done so recently.)

4. What other details in relation to the legal aspects of your marriage do you need to complete? (These may involve children or property.)

Some couples may have other legal arrangements to attend to before the wedding date. These may relate to the establishment of certain property as legally separate, changes in wills or insurance policies, changes in child custody, or other matters that require the aid of an attorney. If you have any concerns in these areas, discuss them with your pastor or with an attorney.

The Wedding Service

Consult with your pastor to arrange for your wedding service, rehearsal (if needed), and related matters. If you have not completed the questionnaires in the back of this book, it will be helpful if you will do so. Some ministers or counselors may offer additional couple-relationship inventories as a part of your preparation for marriage. If you followed the suggestion in chapter 1, you may already have completed some of these matters with your pastor.

Your wedding is a worship service, with its focus upon you and your partner as you express your pledges to each other before God. This can be done well in any type of wedding, whether it is a very simple, informal service with only a few persons present or a large church wedding. Matters of music, ritual, attendants, and other elaborations will be decided by you and your partner in consultation with your officiating minister. He or she often can assist you as you work with relatives and others in arranging the details.

Customs, traditions, and the wishes of parents and others are important considerations. However, with your pastor, you may design your wedding service to express the meanings you want to share. Choose your service on these merits, whether it is a traditional service or an unusual one. Remember to consider the policies of your pastor and church in these arrangements.

Our Concluding Blessing to You

With your partner, you can become more confident with your decisions regarding your relationship as you continue to explore its many facets. Sometimes sincere disagreement and confrontation may be especially helpful as you examine your expectations, improve your communication skills, and establish new goals together. Relatives and friends usually want the best for you, and their suggestions and comments are worth serious consideration, whether you agree with them or not.

We also want you to know that your church is deeply interested in you, your marriage, and your family. If you move from your present church, we encourage you to reestablish your relationship with a local church in your new community. Through your pastor and your church, you have access to many persons and resources. Seek these out and use them effectively to strengthen and develop yourselves and your marriage.

There are many who care for you and your partner as you begin or continue your lives together. As we and the other couples involved in the creation of this guide continue in the adventures of our own marriages, we hope you will experience fulfillment and joy in yours. May you love and cherish each other increasingly, throughout your lives.

For Further Reading

There are many excellent reading resources available from libraries and bookstores, and your minister or counselor can suggest additional helpful materials. Listed here are a few books that you and your partner will find helpful in the areas described.

A. Communication and Problem Solving

Gottman, John; Notarius, Cliff; Gonso, Jonni; and Markman, Howard. *A Couple's Guide to Communication.* Champaign, Ill.: Research Press, 1976.

Contains many helpful exercises as aids in negotiating agreements, dealing with sexual problems, and overcoming crises.

Katz, Mort. *Marriage Survival Kit.* Rockville Centre, N.Y.: Farnsworth Publishing Co., 1975.

Easy-to-read brief descriptions of ways to accept feelings and to grow in marriage. Delightful cartoons and insightful questions provide valuable aids to growing couples.

Miller, Sherod; Nunnally, Elam; and Wackman, Daniel. *Talking Together.* Minneapolis: Interpersonal Communication Programs, 1979.

Provides details of "I messages," an awareness wheel, and ways to improve accurate communication between partners. A workbook also is available.

Narciso, John, and Burkett, David. *Declare Yourself: Discovering the Me in Relationships.* Englewood Cliffs, N.J.: Prentice-Hall, 1975.

After showing how communication can be misused, the authors suggest ways that persons can concentrate on behavior in the present, rather than in the past.

Whitaker, John F. *Personal Marriage Contract.* Dallas, Tex.: OK Street, 1976.

Brief one-page essays on love, friends, rights, time, and other important dimensions of marriage. The "Declaration of Commitment" is well worth reading and discussing.

B. Personal and Family Dynamics, and Parenting

Carr, Jo, and Sorley, Imogene. *The Intentional Family.* Nashville: Abingdon Press, 1971.

Emphasizes the social and religious dimensions of families, with many suggestions to enable couples and families to create and enhance their family life-style and become more committed to growth in Christian love.

Clinebell, Howard J. and Clinebell, Charlotte H. *The Intimate Marriage.* New York: Harper & Row, 1970.

Shows ways to relate personal intimacy in sexual, parenting, and spiritual areas of marriage. Helpful also in viewing positively the changes in marriage across the years.

Gordon, Thomas. *Parent Effectiveness Training.* New York: Peter H. Wyden, 1970.

Oriented toward parents, this book gives more details on "win versus lose" attitudes, "I" and "you" messages, and problem solving.

Gould, Roger L. *Transformations: Growth and Change in Adult Life.* Simon & Schuster, 1978.

An insightful discussion of ways to achieve personal growth during the young-adult and middle-adult years. Among the many emotional areas are two-career marriages, separation from parents, achievement of independence, and the ability to cope with death.

Laing, R. D. *Knots.* New York: Vintage, Random House, 1970.

Poems that describe the emotional and psychological systems of families. Difficult, but well worth discussing with your partner.

C. Finances and Careers

Bolles, Richard N. *What Color Is Your Parachute?* Berkeley, Cal.: Ten Speed Press, 1972.

Provides perspectives and guides for persons who want to locate a career they will enjoy and that can lead to personal growth.

Household Finance Corporation. *Planning Your Spending.* Bulletin no. 4, 1978.

Contains details of money management, budgeting, and suggested expenditure patterns.

Porter, Sylvia. *Sylvia Porter's New Money Book for the 80's.* New York: Doubleday & Co., 1979.

Offers many suggestions for personal finance that can be applied in several areas of marriage.

D. Human Sexuality

Masters, W. H. and Johnson, Virginia. *The Pleasure Bond: A New Look at Sexuality and Commitment.* Boston: Little, Brown & Co., 1975.

> Based on their extensive research in human sexual functioning, these authors provide details that can guide couples in the better sharing of their love through sexual activities.

McCary, James L. *Human Sexuality: Physiological, Psychological, and Sociological Factors.* New York: Van Nostrand Reinhold Co., 1977.

> Provides accurate information about all areas of human sexual functioning.

Nelson, James. *Embodiment: An Approach to Sexuality and Christian Theology.* Augsburg Publishing House, 1978.

> A serious, careful theological discussion of human sexuality.

E. Marriage Enrichment

Clinebell, Howard J., Jr. *Growth Counseling for Marriage Enrichment.* Philadelphia: Fortress Press, 1975.

> Designed for pastors and for couples who would like to enrich their marriages through group experiences, this book contains suggestions for a variety of marriage enhancement programs.

Hunt, Joan, and Hunt, Richard. *MIRROR: Couple Relationship Inventory.* Dallas, Tex.: Datascan, Inc., 1981.

> Provides a way for couples to examine concepts of selves and partners. Deals with strengths, communication skills, attitudes, and other areas related to marriage. For pastors and for couples. Available from Datascan, P.O. Box 8265, Dallas TX 75205.

Mace, David, and Mace, Vera. *How to Have a Happy Marriage.* Nashville: Abingdon, 1977.

> Offers many practical suggestions for beginning and continuing a satisfying marriage from a growth perspective.

————. *We Can Have Better Marriages If We Really Want Them.* Nashville: Abingdon Press, 1974.

> Written by the founders of the Association of Couples for Marriage Enrichment (ACME), this brief volume shows how partners can grow in marriage and how couples can work together to strengthen marriage and family life in today's society.

————. *Marriage Enrichment in the Church.* Nashville: Broadman Press, 1977.

> Describes the possibilities and some available procedures for a variety of marriage enrichment sessions.

F. Textbooks on Marriage and the Family

Duvall, Evelyn M. *Family Development.* 5th ed. Philadelphia: J. B. Lippincott Co., 1977.

Hunt, R. A. and Rydman, E. J. *Creative Marriage.* 2nd ed. Boston: Allyn & Bacon, 1979.

McCary, James L. *Freedom and Growth in Marriage.* Hamilton, Ohio: Wiley, 1975.

Smith, Rebecca M. *Klemer's Marriage and Family Relationships.* New York: Harper & Row, 1975.

WEDDING INFORMATION

(Appropriate information is to be filled in by the couple together. Dates should be set in consultation with pastor.)

Woman's full name _____

Address _____

Telephone at work _____ Home _____

Parents' Name _____

Address _____

Man's full name _____

Address _____

Telephone at work _____ Home _____

Parents' Name _____

Address _____

Your address after wedding _____

Dates for premarital conferences with pastor: Couple _____

Man _____ Woman _____ Couple _____

Dates for premarital conferences with physician:

Man _____ Woman _____

Physician's name(s) _____

Have you secured the marriage license? _____

If not, when? _____

Rehearsal Date _____ Hour _____ Place _____

Rehearsal Dinner _____ Hour _____ Place _____

Wedding Date _____ Hour _____

Place _____

Maid of Honor _____

Best Man _____

Bridesmaids _____

_____

_____

Ushers _____

_____

_____

Other attendants _____

_____

_____

Who presents the bride in marriage? _____

Will you use one ring? _____ or two rings? _____

Where will the reception be held? _____ Hour? _____

Organist _____

Soloist _____

Florist _____

Photographer _____

REMOVE ALONG DOTTED LINE

PREMARITAL QUESTIONNAIRE[1]

(To be filled in by man alone)

Pastor will assign:

Man's _____   Woman's _____
Code Number _____   Code Number _____

Date _____   Place _____

Answer all questions (without partner's help). CIRCLE NUMBER in front of appropriate response, or FILL IN BLANKS.

1. Your age _____   Partner's age _____

2. Your birthplace _____
   Father's _____   Mother's _____

3. What is your present marital status?
   1 Single   2 Divorced: Date? _____
   3 Widowed: Date? _____   4 Other (specify) _____

4. If you have children, gives ages. Boys _____   Girls _____

5. In what religion were you brought up?
   _____   Partner _____
   In what religion are you now active?
   _____   Partner _____

6. Write in highest number of years of school or college completed (not including vocational training). _____   Partner _____
   Write in kinds of vocational training:
   Partner _____

7. Did you share in the housework when you were growing up?
   1 No   2 Occasionally   3 Frequently
   Do you like housework?
   1 Very much   2 Somewhat   3 Dislike

8. If your mother worked for pay while you were growing up, what was her occupation(s)? _____
   How did you feel about it?
   1 Liked   2 Disliked   3 Mixed feelings

9. What was your father's occupation(s) as you were growing up? _____

10. What is your occupation? _____
    Partner's _____

11. What was your order of birth?
    1 Only child   2 Youngest   3 Oldest   4 In between
    Ages of living brothers _____   Sisters _____

12. How happy were you while growing up?
    1 Very happy   2 Happy   3 Unhappy   4 Very unhappy
    How did (do) you feel about yourself as a person?

Before teens	During teens	Now
1 Very well	1 Very well	1 Very well
2 Fairly well	2 Fairly well	2 Fairly well
3 Poorly	3 Poorly	3 Poorly
4 Uncertain	4 Uncertain	4 Uncertain

13. When you were 16 or 17, how many boyfriends did you have?
    1 Very few   2 Some   3 Many
    How many girlfriends did you have?
    1 Very few   2 Some   3 Many

14. What is the present marital status of your parents?
    1 Married, living together   6 Divorced, both remarried
    2 Separated, marital friction   7 Widowed, not remarried
    3 Divorced, neither remarried   8 Widowed, remarried
    4 Divorced, mother remarried   9 Neither living
    5 Divorced, father remarried   0 Other (specify) _____
    If your parents' marriage was broken by death, divorce, or separation, how old were you at the time? _____

15. How would you describe your parents' (substitutes') relationship?
    1 Warmly affectionate   2 Affectionate, reserved
    3 No affection
    Comment: _____
    To what extent did (do) they agree? disagree?
    1 In conflict all the time   2 Alternately fighting, making up
    3 Tolerated without conflict   4 Few conflicts apparent
    How happy was (is) their marriage?
    1 Very happy   2 Happy   3 Unhappy   4 Very unhappy

[1]Adapted with permission from Background and Schedule E forms of the Marriage Council of Philadelphia, Inc.

16. How did (do) you get along with your mother (substitute)?

Before teens	During teens	Now
1 Very well	1 Very well	1 Very well
2 Fairly well	2 Fairly well	2 Fairly well
3 Poorly	3 Poorly	3 Poorly
4 Not apply	4 Not apply	4 Not apply

How did (do) you get along with your father (substitute)?

Before teens	During teens	Now
1 Very well	1 Very well	1 Very well
2 Fairly well	2 Fairly well	2 Fairly well
3 Poorly	3 Poorly	3 Poorly
4 Not apply	4 Not apply	4 Not apply

Did(do) you get along with one parent better than the other?

Before teens	During teens	Now
1 Mother better	1 Mother better	1 Mother better
2 Father better	2 Father better	2 Father better
3 Both same	3 Both same	3 Both same
4 Not apply	4 Not apply	4 Not apply

17. What is your relationship to your partner?

1 Formal engagement 2 Engagement without announcement

3 Informal agreement 4 Other (specify) _____

Date of engagement _____ Wedding Date _____

18. Were you ever engaged to anyone else?

1 No 2 Once 3 Two or more times

19. How long have you known your partner?

_____ years _____ months

20. Have you and your partner ever temporarily broken your relationship?

1 No 2 Once 3 Two or more times

21. Have you been separated by military service, school, work, etc.?

1 No 2 Yes How long? _____

How do you feel this separation affected your relationship?

1 Helped 2 Hurt 3 No effect

22. Do you confide in your partner? 1 Helped 2 Hurt 3 No effect

How does your partner feel? 1 Most things 2 Few things

Does your partner confide in you? 1 Most things 2 Few things

23. Do these people (if living) approve of your marriage?

	Yes	No	Not sure (explain)
Mother (substitute)	_____	_____	_____
Father (substitute)	_____	_____	_____

24. How do you get along with your future in-laws (substitutes)?

	Yes	No	Not sure (explain)
Future mother-in-law	_____	_____	_____
Future father-in-law	_____	_____	_____

Father-in-law	Mother-in-law
1 Very well	1 Very well
2 Fairly well	2 Fairly well
3 Poorly	3 Poorly
4 Have not met	4 Have not met

How does your partner get along with your parents (substitutes)?

Father	Mother
1 Very well	1 Very well
2 Fairly well	2 Fairly well
3 Poorly	3 Poorly
4 Has not met	4 Has not met

How does your partner get along with your own parents (substitutes)?

Father	Mother
1 Very well	1 Very well
2 Fairly well	2 Fairly well
3 Poorly	3 Poorly
4 Has not met	4 Has not met

25. After marriage, where will you live?

1 Do not know 2 By ourselves

3 With parents, in-laws 4 With others (specify) _____

26. Will both work for pay?

1 No 2 Yes How long? _____

27. Have you planned your budget?

1 No 2 Yes 3 Are discussing

Will your earned income be supplemented by other resources?

1 No 2 Yes, parents or in-laws

3 Other (specify) _____

Will you and your partner give financial support to others?

1 No 2 Yes (specify) _____

28. How do you and your partner expect to divide responsibility for home activities? (Write "H" for husband; "W" for wife; "HW" for mainly husband with wife's help, or vice versa; "E" for equally.)

Daily household tasks	_____	Maintenance activities	_____
Buying food, supplies	_____	Child care	_____
Handling money	_____	Other (specify)	_____

29. In what activities do you and your partner take part? (Write "H" for husband and "W" for wife for each activity.)

	None	Little	Some	Much
Movies				
Dances				
Competitive sports (tennis, etc.)				
Spectator sports (football, etc.)				
Outdoor activities (walking, fishing, etc.)				
Social gatherings with friends				
Church (church school, etc.)				
Service activities				
Politics				
Reading				
Art appreciation (music, paintings, etc.)				
Creative art (writing, acting, etc.)				
Hobbies (collecting, sewing, etc.)				
Membership in clubs, organizations				
Business activities (beyond work hours)				

How do you feel about this sharing of interests and activities?
1 Satisfied 2 Desire less 3 Desire more 4 Not sure
How does your partner feel about this sharing?
1 Satisfied 2 Desires less 3 Desires more 4 Not sure

30. How much affection do you show partner (kissing, embracing)?
1 Little 2 Some 3 Much
Are you satisfied with the amount of affection?
1 Yes 2 Desire less 3 Desire more 4 Not sure
Is your partner satisfied with the amount of affection?
1 Yes 2 Desires less 3 Desires more 4 Do not know

31. Have you obtained information from courses, reading, or counseling that has helped you understand sexual relations?
1 No 2 Yes
List most helpful _____

32. Did your parents (substitutes) discuss sex with you?
1 No 2 Yes, freely 3 With reserve
How helpful were these discussions?
1 Helpful 2 Harmful 3 No effect

33. How do you think your mother (substitute) feels or felt about sex?
1 Happy 2 Tolerating 3 Rejecting 4 Do not know
How do you think your father (substitute) feels or felt about sex?
1 Happy 2 Tolerating 3 Rejecting 4 Do not know

34. How do you anticipate sexual relations in marriage?
1 With pleasure 2 With mixed feelings
3 With dislike 4 Somewhat fearfully
Do you consider your knowledge of sex adequate for marriage?
1 Yes 2 No 3 Doubtful
Do you feel the need for additional help in any of these areas?
1 Sex play 2 Intercourse 3 Response of opposite sex
4 Attitudes 5 Child spacing 6 Help for partner
7 Other (specify) _____

35. Have you decided to have children?
1 No 2 Yes 3 Are discussing
How many do you want? _____ Your partner? _____
How soon after marriage do you expect to have children? _____

36. Disagreements with partner usually result in
1 Agreement by mutual give and take 2 My giving in
3 Partner giving in 4 Neither giving in
When disagreements arise, we usually
1 Settle them quickly and easily 2 Never settle them
3 Struggle over them a long time 4 No disagreements

37. How confident are you that your marriage will be happy?
1 Very confident 2 Fairly confident
3 Little uncertain 4 Very uncertain
Explain _____

38. Have you had disagreement over these items? (For each item, put two check marks, one on each side of the heavy line.)

Item	None; not arisen	None; we agreed	Little	Some	Much	Discussed in depth	Discussed superficially
	Check One					Check One	
Mother							
Father							
Mother-in-law to be							
Father-in-law to be							
Other relatives							
Personal habits							
Health							
Wife's work							
Husband's work							
Where to live							
Household management							
Finances							
Religion							
Values, life goals							
Political, social issues							
Education							
Social background							
Friends							
Recreation							
Community activities							
Communication							
Sexual relations							
Jealousy							
Personality							
Children							
Other							

39. Comments:

REMOVE ALONG DOTTED LINE

PREMARITAL QUESTIONNAIRE[1]
(To be filled in by woman alone)

Pastor will assign:
Woman's
Code Number _____

Man's
Code Number _____

Date _____ Place _____

Answer all questions (without partner's help). CIRCLE NUMBER in front of appropriate response, or FILL IN BLANKS.

1. Your age _____ Partner's age _____
2. Your birthplace _____
   Father's _____ Mother's _____
3. What is your present marital status?
   1 Single 2 Divorced: Date? _____
   3 Widowed: Date? _____ 4 Other (specify) _____
4. If you have children, gives ages. Boys _____ Girls _____
5. In what religion were you brought up?
   Partner _____
   In what religion are you now active? _____
   Partner _____
6. Write in highest number of years of school or college completed (not including vocational training). _____ Partner _____
   Write in kinds of vocational training: _____
   Partner _____
7. Did you share in the housework when you were growing up?
   1 No 2 Occasionally 3 Frequently
   Do you like housework?
   1 Very much 2 Somewhat 3 Dislike
8. If your mother worked for pay while you were growing up, what was her occupation(s)? _____
   How did you feel about it?
   1 Liked 2 Disliked 3 Mixed feelings
9. What was your father's occupation(s) as you were growing up? _____
10. What is your occupation? _____
    Partner's _____
11. What was your order of birth?
    1 Only child 2 Youngest 3 Oldest 4 In between
    Ages of living brothers _____ Sisters _____

12. How happy were you while growing up?
    1 Very happy 2 Happy 3 Unhappy 4 Very unhappy
    How did (do) you feel about yourself as a person?

Before teens	During teens	Now
1 Very well	1 Very well	1 Very well
2 Fairly well	2 Fairly well	2 Fairly well
3 Poorly	3 Poorly	3 Poorly
4 Uncertain	4 Uncertain	4 Uncertain

13. When you were 16 or 17, how many boyfriends did you have?
    1 Very few 2 Some 3 Many
    How many girlfriends did you have?
    1 Very few 2 Some 3 Many
14. What is the present marital status of your parents?
    1 Married, living together 6 Divorced, both remarried
    2 Separated, marital friction 7 Widowed, not remarried
    3 Divorced, neither remarried 8 Widowed, remarried
    4 Divorced, mother remarried 9 Neither living
    5 Divorced, father remarried 0 Other (specify) _____
    If your parents' marriage was broken by death, divorce, or separation, how old were you at the time? _____
15. How would you describe your parents' (substitutes') relationship?
    1 Warmly affectionate 2 Affectionate, reserved
    3 No affection
    Comment: _____
    To what extent did (do) they agree? disagree?
    1 In conflict all the time 2 Alternately fighting, making up
    3 Tolerated without conflict 4 Few conflicts apparent
    How happy was (is) their marriage?
    1 Very happy 2 Happy 3 Unhappy 4 Very unhappy

[1]Adapted with permission from *Background* and *Schedule E* forms of the Marriage Council of Philadelphia, Inc.

88

16. How did (do) you get along with your mother (substitute)?

	Before teens	During teens	Now
1	Very well	1 Very well	1 Very well
2	Fairly well	2 Fairly well	2 Fairly well
3	Poorly	3 Poorly	3 Poorly
4	Not apply	4 Not apply	4 Not apply

How did (do) you get along with your father (substitute)?

	Before teens	During teens	Now
1	Very well	1 Very well	1 Very well
2	Fairly well	2 Fairly well	2 Fairly well
3	Poorly	3 Poorly	3 Poorly
4	Not apply	4 Not apply	4 Not apply

Did(do) you get along with one parent better than the other?

	Before teens	During teens	Now
1	Mother better	1 Mother better	1 Mother better
2	Father better	2 Father better	2 Father better
3	Both same	3 Both same	3 Both same
4	Not apply	4 Not apply	4 Not apply

17. What is your relationship to your partner?
1 Formal engagement 2 Engagement without announcement
3 Informal agreement 4 Other (specify) _____
Date of engagement _____ Wedding Date _____

18. Were you ever engaged to anyone else?
1 No 2 Once 3 Two or more times

19. How long have you known your partner? _____ months

20. Have you and your partner ever temporarily broken your relationship?
1 No 2 Once 3 Two or more times

21. Have you been separated by military service, school, work, etc.?
1 No 2 Yes How long? _____
How do you feel this separation affected your relationship?
1 Helped 2 Hurt 3 No effect
How does your partner feel? 1 Helped 2 Hurt 3 No effect

22. Do you confide in your partner? 1 Most things 2 Few things
Does your partner confide in you? 1 Most things 2 Few things

23. Do these people (if living) approve of your marriage?

	Yes	No	Not sure (explain)
Mother (substitute)	_____		
Father (substitute)	_____		

24. How do you get along with your future in-laws (substitutes)?

Father-in-law	Mother-in-law
1 Very well	1 Very well
2 Fairly well	2 Fairly well
3 Poorly	3 Poorly
4 Have not met	4 Have not met

How does your partner get along with your parents (substitutes)?

Father	Mother
1 Very well	1 Very well
2 Fairly well	2 Fairly well
3 Poorly	3 Poorly
4 Has not met	4 Has not met

How does your partner get along with own parents (substitutes)?

Father	Mother
1 Very well	1 Very well
2 Fairly well	2 Fairly well
3 Poorly	3 Poorly
4 Has not met	4 Has not met

25. After marriage, where will you live?
1 Do not know 2 By ourselves
3 With parents, in-laws 4 With others (specify) _____

26. Will both work for pay?
1 No 2 Yes How long? _____

27. Have you planned your budget?
1 No 2 Yes 3 Are discussing
Will your earned income be supplemented by other resources?
1 No 2 Yes, parents or in-laws
3 Other (specify) _____
Will you and your partner give financial support to others?
1 No 2 Yes (specify) _____

28. How do you and your partner expect to divide responsibility for home activities? (Write "H" for husband; "W" for wife; "H/W" for mainly husband with wife's help, or vice versa; "E" for equally.)

Daily household tasks	_____	Maintenance activities	_____
Buying food, supplies	_____	Child care	_____
Handling money	_____	Other (specify)	_____

Future mother-in-law _____ Yes No Not sure (explain)
Future father-in-law _____

29. In what activities do you and your partner take part? (Write "H" for husband and "W" for wife for each activity.)

	None	Little	Some	Much
Movies				
Dances				
Competitive sports (tennis, etc.)				
Spectator sports (football, etc.)				
Outdoor activities (walking, fishing, etc.)				
Social gatherings with friends				
Church (church school, etc.)				
Service activities				
Politics				
Reading				
Art appreciation (music, paintings, etc.)				
Creative art (writing, acting, etc.)				
Hobbies (collecting, sewing, etc.)				
Membership in clubs, organizations				
Business activities (beyond work hours)				

How do you feel about this sharing of interests and activities?
1 Satisfied   2 Desire less   3 Desire more   4 Not sure
How does your partner feel about this sharing?
1 Satisfied   2 Desires less   3 Desires more   4 Not sure

30. How much affection do you show partner (kissing, embracing)?
1 Little   2 Some   3 Much
Are you satisfied with the amount of affection?
1 Yes   2 Desire less   3 Desire more   4 Not sure
Is your partner satisfied with the amount of affection?
1 Yes   2 Desires less   3 Desires more   4 Do not know

31. Have you obtained information from courses, reading, or counseling that has helped you understand sexual relations?
1 No   2 Yes
List most helpful _____

32. Did your parents (substitutes) discuss sex with you?
1 No   2 Yes, freely   3 With reserve
How helpful were these discussions?
1 Helpful   2 Harmful   3 No effect

33. How do you think your mother (substitute) feels or felt about sex?
1 Happy   2 Tolerating   3 Rejecting   4 Do not know
How do you think your father (substitute) feels or felt about sex?
1 Happy   2 Tolerating   3 Rejecting   4 Do not know

34. How do you anticipate sexual relations in marriage?
1 With pleasure   2 With mixed feelings
3 With dislike   4 Somewhat fearfully
Do you consider your knowledge of sex adequate for marriage?
1 Yes   2 No   3 Doubtful
Do you feel the need for additional help in any of these areas?
1 Sex play   2 Intercourse   3 Response of opposite sex
4 Attitudes   5 Child spacing   6 Help for partner
7 Other (specify) _____

35. Have you decided to have children?
1 No   2 Yes   3 Are discussing
How many do you want? _____ Your partner? _____
How soon after marriage do you expect to have children? _____

36. Disagreements with partner usually result in
1 Agreement by mutual give and take   2 My giving in
3 Partner giving in   4 Neither giving in
When disagreements arise, we usually
1 Settle them quickly and easily   2 Never settle them
3 Struggle over them a long time   4 No disagreements

37. How confident are you that your marriage will be happy?
1 Very confident   2 Fairly confident
3 Little uncertain   4 Very uncertain
Explain: _____
_____
_____

38. Have you had disagreement over these items? (For each item, put two check marks, one on each side of the heavy line.)

	Check One					Check One	
	None; not arisen	None; we agreed	Little	Some	Much	Discussed in depth	Discussed superficially
Mother							
Father							
Mother-in-law to be							
Father-in-law to be							
Other relatives							
Personal habits							
Health							
Wife's work							
Husband's work							
Where to live							
Household management							
Finances							
Religion							
Values, life goals							
Political, social issues							
Education							
Social background							
Friends							
Recreation							
Community activities							
Communication							
Sexual relations							
Jealousy							
Personality							
Children							
Other							

39. Comments:

Note: This is a duplicate of the form on page 18. Read instructions in that chapter before using this form.

Place a mark on each line to indicate the point at which you see yourself and another mark for the point at which you see your partner on each dimension. To aid your comparisons later, use this code:

F = Female's view of self   M = Male's view of self
H = Female's view of man (Husband)   W = Male's view of woman (Wife)

sometimes insecure___:___:___:___:___:___:___very confident
likes to control___:___:___:___:___:___:___likes to be controlled
very warm and caring___:___:___:___:___:___:___cool, distant
pessimistic, sad___:___:___:___:___:___:___happy, optimistic
active___:___:___:___:___:___:___quiet
gives in, passive___:___:___:___:___:___:___demanding, aggressive
tense___:___:___:___:___:___:___relaxed
open, flexible___:___:___:___:___:___:___unbending, closed
likes being with others___:___:___:___:___:___:___likes being alone
likes to listen___:___:___:___:___:___:___likes to talk
withholds affection___:___:___:___:___:___:___always very affectionate

Compare your answers on the two sheets, or transfer those responses to this sheet with a different color pen or pencil.

REMOVE ALONG DOTTED LINE

Note: This is a duplicate of the form on page 20. Read instructions in that chapter before using this form.

Use this checklist to show how you feel about each other's habits. Answer separately, and after you finish, compare answers.

	Very Bothered	Sometimes Bothered	Usually Neutral	Sometimes Pleased	Very Pleased
punctuality	———	———	———	———	———
appearance, dress, grooming	———	———	———	———	———
forgetfulness	———	———	———	———	———
suggestions my partner gives	———	———	———	———	———
attention my partner gives me when we are with others	———	———	———	———	———
use of tobacco	———	———	———	———	———
use of alcoholic beverages	———	———	———	———	———
use of drugs; medications	———	———	———	———	———
driving habits	———	———	———	———	———
sense of humor	———	———	———	———	———
expressions of affection	———	———	———	———	———
housekeeping, neatness	———	———	———	———	———
openness, flexibility	———	———	———	———	———
honesty, truthfulness	———	———	———	———	———
respect for others; for me	———	———	———	———	———
care of property, belongings	———	———	———	———	———
money habits	———	———	———	———	———
encouragement of me	———	———	———	———	———
cooperation, consideration	———	———	———	———	———
conversational skills	———	———	———	———	———
speech: swearing, jargon	———	———	———	———	———
sleep habits	———	———	———	———	———
daily scheduling	———	———	———	———	———
food and eating habits	———	———	———	———	———

Note: This is a duplicate of the form on page 35. Read instructions in that chapter before using this form.

Rate yourself and your partner in the appropriate columns. The statements are phrased to apply to either partner, as sender and as receiver of messages in the taped conversa- tion. After responding to the statements, you and your partner can compare your judgments. Use the following code:

1 = not *aware of this in my taped conversation*
2 = *aware of this but did not do it at all*
3 = *did this some but could have done it more*
4 = *did this well, satisfactorily*
5 = *did this very well, as often as needed*

Rating of

WOMAN	MAN	WHEN PERSON *SENT* MESSAGES (PERSON AS SENDER)
——	——	1. *Sender was completely clear about message to be sent.*
——	——	2. *Sender checked with listener to be sure she or he was ready for message before sending it.*
——	——	3. *Sender used words that had same meaning for listener as for sender.*
——	——	4. *Sender stopped speaking occasionally to be sure listener was receiving accurate message.*
——	——	5. *Sender was open to feedback and encouraged listener to ask that message be repeated or clarified.*
——	——	6. *Sender easily distinguished between his or her message and the reactions of the listener to the message.*

WOMAN	MAN	WHEN PERSON *RECEIVED* MESSAGES (PERSON AS RECEIVER, LISTENER)
——	——	1. *Listener encouraged sender by being willing to listen.*
——	——	2. *Listener turned and faced sending partner, looked at him or her.*
——	——	3. *Listener put other thoughts aside and gave full attention to sender and message.*
——	——	4. *Listener placed own emotional reactions aside in order to become fully aware of partner's feelings and meanings.*
——	——	5. *Listener summarized message as feedback, so that sender could confirm accuracy of listener's understanding of message.*
——	——	6. *When message was unclear or came too fast, listener stopped sender and asked him or her to repeat or clarify message.*
——	——	7. *When sender paused or was unable to find "the exact word," listener waited patiently, speaking only if requested.*
——	——	8. *Listener kept sender informed of listening levels by informing sender when he or she wanted to give feedback, send a reply, or continue to receive more messages.*

REMOVE ALONG DOTTED LINE

73726

Note: This is a duplicate of the form on page 37. Read instructions in that chapter before using this form.

*Separately, put a check or X beside the **eight** words that best describe your own responses in times of disagreement between you and your partner. Answer as you see yourself.*

SHE	HE	TYPE OF RESPONSE		SHE	HE	TYPE OF RESPONSE
——	——	1. withdraws		——	——	11. threatens
——	——	2. negotiates		——	——	12. pretends
——	——	3. gives in		——	——	13. looks openly at issues
——	——	4. forces own way		——	——	14. retreats, hides from issue
——	——	5. clarifies		——	——	15. begrudges, resentful
——	——	6. becomes silent		——	——	16. leaves room, vacates
——	——	7. blames someone		——	——	17. pressures, pushes
——	——	8. explains		——	——	18. surrenders
——	——	9. criticizes		——	——	19. disappears
——	——	10. evades the issue		——	——	20. compromises